STORIES OF LONG AGO
NIIHAU • KAUAI • OAHU

Ida Elizabeth Knudsen von Holt
1868–1941

STORIES OF LONG AGO
NIIHAU • KAUAI • OAHU

by
IDA ELIZABETH KNUDSEN VON HOLT

Revised Edition
1985

Published by Daughters of Hawaii
HONOLULU

Copyright © 1985 Daughters of Hawaii
All rights reserved
Privately printed in 1953 and 1968
by Star-Bulletin Printing Company, Honolulu
Paperback edition by Daughters of Hawaii, 1985
Second printing, 1986

The Daughters of Hawaii have chosen to publish the text of this book as it was written despite any possible historical inaccuracies. Some new material has been included to add interest to the book.

Cover watercolor: *Pastures and Taro Patches* by Maude Knudsen Garstin, 1898. A view of Niihau from Waimea, Kauai.

DEDICATION

To my husband, Harry Martens von Holt
and for my children and grandchildren

CONTENTS

The Sinclair Clan	1
The Life at Craigforth	16
The Voyage of the Bessie	27
The Saga of Valdemar Knudsen	44
Waiawa	68
The Anglo-Germanic Alliance	98
"Na Olelo o Ita me Hale"	122
Ida Elizabeth Knudsen von Holt (From the *Hawaiian Church Chronicle*, July 1941)	155
Appendix	157
Genealogy Chart	160–161

ILLUSTRATIONS

Ida Elizabeth Knudsen von Holt	Frontis
Craigforth	17
Kiekie, Niihau	34
Mrs. Francis Sinclair and Family	37
Knud Knudsen	47
Anne Sinclair	64
Valdemar Knudsen	65
Makaweli House	72
Knudsen Family Group	74
Kii Landing, Niihau	76
Garstin Watercolor Paintings	follows page 82
Anne Sinclair Knudsen	96
Thomas Brown	100
Mary Ann Rhodes Brown	101
Alice Brown and Hermann von Holt	105
Alice Brown von Holt with Harry	107
Margaretha Martens	108
Johann Hinrich Martens	109
Alice Mackintosh with Children	112
Family Group at Sunnyslope	114
Harry Martens von Holt	127
Ida Elizabeth Knudsen	129
Ida and Harry von Holt with Herman and Mary	137
Harry Martens von Holt Family	139
Twenty-nine B	144
Pa Lehua	145
Kikila	152

ACKNOWLEDGEMENTS

The Daughters of Hawaii are indebted to the von Holt family for their donation of the rights to *"Stories of Long Ago,"* now publicly printed for the first time. It seems appropriate that the Daughters of Hawaii publish this book as there are now thirty five active members that are descendents of the families whose lives are traced in these stories.

Ida von Holt was one of the early members of the Daughters of Hawaii, which was founded in 1903 by seven women who were daughters of American Protestant missionaries. They foresaw the inevitable loss of much of the Hawaiian culture and founded the organization "to perpetuate the memory and spirit of old Hawaii and of historic events, and to preserve the nomenclature and correct pronunciation of the Hawaiian language." Membership is open to any woman who is directly descended from a person who lived in Hawaii prior to 1880, with no restriction to race.

The Daughters of Hawaii maintain and operate Queen Emma Summer Palace in Honolulu and Hulihee Palace in Kailua-Kona on the island of Hawaii. Income for operations is derived from admission, membership dues, fund raising activities and donations. The society is a non-profit corporation managed by a volunteer board of trustees.

The following contributors to the publication of this book are gratefully acknowledged.

Mary E. von Holt White
Mr. and Mrs. Reynolds G. Burkland
Mr. and Mrs. Robert E. White, Jr.
Cecil Brown Trust
Geoffrey R. v. H. Chapman
Ruth Knudsen Hanner
Mr. and Mrs. Robert R. Midkiff
Mr. and Mrs. Herman V. von Holt
Katharine A. von Holt Caldwell
Mr. and Mrs. Thomas D. Perkins
Mr. and Mrs. Robert B. Marchant
Matthew P. S. Chapman
Cynthia Garstin Blackwell
Mr. and Mrs. James Jordan
Ida I. Perkins

CHAPTER I

The Sinclair Clan

AMONG my earliest memories are the fascinating and romantic stories told me by my mother, Anne Sinclair Knudsen, of her early life, and that of her father and mother, Captain and Mistress Francis Sinclair.

My grandmother, Elizabeth or "Eliza" McHutchison was born in Glasgow, Scotland on April 26, 1800. Her father was one of the leading citizens, and well known for his entertainments. The home in Glasgow was large and beautifully furnished, and attached to it, and extending the length of the house, was an aviary which was renowned over the country and a constant source of pleasure to the family and friends. After the grand dinners, when the ladies had been sent home in their sedan chairs, the Lord Provost and the other gentlemen would remain drinking. It was not considered a proper entertainment unless they were so overcome they would fall under the table. In the early mornings Elizabeth, as a child, would see them walking about in the garden to recover themselves before going home.

Elizabeth was a beautiful girl, about five feet in height. She had regular features, and lovely wide-set deep blue eyes. There were six in the family, and as children they were fed on simple food. All they had for breakfast was oatmeal porridge and milk. The porridge was poured out into a plate, then "set" for a few minutes to "jell over." No Scotch child ever had anything else even if he did not want to eat it. Off to school at 8 o'clock, they would return ravenously hungry for their plain midday dinner; and for supper they would have bread and milk.

That Elizabeth thrived on it was proven by her abounding good health. She always enjoyed the story of an Englishman who was making fun of the Scotch, saying: "Why we only feed our horses on oats." Quietly a Scotchmen present replied, "Yes, and look at your horses."

Elizabeth's father was evidently proud of his daughters; it is said he supervised every detail of their ball dresses. When the girls came to him dressed in their pretty frocks, he would measure with his forefinger the length between the low bodice in the front and the high waist line "to see if the dress were low enough." If it proved more than a finger's length, the fashionable cut in those days, he would have it altered.

When Elizabeth was eighteen she made her debut, and was famous as one of the beauties of Glasgow. She was evidently her father's favorite, and often accompanied him on his business trips. It was on one of these that she first met my grandfather, Captain Francis Sinclair of the Royal Navy.

He was born in Edinburgh, Scotland, the son of Sir George Sinclair, and belonged to the Sinclair Clan of which the head carried the title of the Earl of Caithness until 1920.

I think a dip into ancient history will prove interesting at this point of my story of the Sinclairs and St. Clairs.

While in Scotland in 1936 I was most fortunately rewarded in my search for the history of the Sinclair Clan by being advised of a small booklet about the family and the Charters from which I quote:

"A certain Father Richard Hay, Prior of St. Pieremont, whose mother was married to Sir James St. Clair of Rosslyn, has left the only authentic information about the family of St. Clairs.

"Being of an antiquarian turn of mind he made use of the opportunity afforded him of examining the various Charters in possession of the family about the year 1700. These notes of the Charters were published in 1835 under the title of *Genealogy of the Saint-Clairs of Rosslyn including the Chartu-*

lary of Rosslyn. This was fortunate as a fire in the Castle later destroyed all the old Charters and papers.

"The family descended from one Woldonius who took the name of Saint Claire from the place, probably in Normandy, where his estate was situated. He married a daughter of Richard Duke of Normandy, father of William the Conqueror, and their son William accompanied his uncle the Conqueror to England and fought in the battle of Hastings in 1066. Soon after that this William Saint-Clair went to Scotland and served under the Scottish King Malcom Canmore. His grandson was 'dubbed' a Knight by King David I, about 1138. The family was true to the Scotch tradition and served under the Kings—Malcom, David and The Bruce."

The title, Earl of Caithness, from which our branch descended was first mentioned in 1358; and in 1481 the records show the first mention of the name as spelled Sinclair. A Baron Sinclair was declared by Act of Parliament to be the Chief of the St. Clairs. It seems that the name of St. Clair was interchangeable in spelling with Sinclair.

In 1471 the estates of the powerful family were scattered among their sons who formed three branches of the family:
   The Lords St. Clair of Dysart
   The St. Clairs of Rosslyn, and
   The Sinclairs of Caithness, whose title,
Earl of Caithness, went to each succeeding eldest son.

In 1883 my uncle, Francis Sinclair, who was then living at his beautiful home "The Pines" on Mt. Eden in Auckland, New Zealand, heard of the death without heir of the reigning earl. Though he knew he was next of kin, he did not let himself be known, even though the English and Scotch papers advertised widely for an heir to come forward. He had previously been up in the north of Scotland, and seen the estate near Aberdeen. As the fine castle Dunbeath was going to ruin, and he had no children, he did not wish to assume the responsibilities of the title, and make his home in that part of Scotland. A cousin of the late earl, a barrister in London, was found and proved next of kin and took the title. He died in 1920 in Hollywood, California, without heirs, and was the last Earl of Caithness of our immediate Sinclair Clan. My mother, Anne Sinclair Knudsen, who was living in Hollywood at that time, went to the funeral and put flowers on his grave.

The present representative of our Sinclair Clan is Sir Archibald Sinclair, member of Parliament, and a clever forceful man.

The Sinclair Clan has two patterns in their Tartan, one a red and green in large checks and one called the Hunting Tartan, a lovely one of green with hair line checks of green and white and red.

When on my third visit to Scotland in 1936, the young lady in charge of the guide-map and post-card shop was interested at once when I quoted Sir Walter Scott's words, which I often heard my mother repeat: "And each St. Clair is buried there with Rood and Book and Knell." When I told her my mother was a Sinclair of the Caithness clan she smiled and remarked, "You perhaps don't know that the two branches are jokingly called the Saints and the Sinners." I was much amused but assured her I was very proud to belong to "the Sinners."

To return to the story of my grandfather, Captain Sinclair of the Royal Navy. He was over six feet two inches in height and was said to be the handsomest man in Scotland. His dark curly hair was worn without a queue, a style which was just coming into fashion.

In 1815 after the decisive battle of Waterloo he had the honor of bringing the Duke of Wellington from Belgium over to England in his frigate of war. When off the cliffs of Dover, a sudden squall hit the vessel. It was only Captain Sinclair's quick action at the tiller that saved the ship from going on the rocks. The great "Iron Duke" was on the deck watching the whole scene, and after the ship had been safely brought into the harbor he expressed himself warmly, thanking Captain Sinclair for saving his life. Some weeks after this my grandfather received a beautiful folding desk with a silver plate on it with the following inscription: "To Captain Francis Sinclair, in token of his splendid seamanship, and the gratitude and esteem of the Duke of Wellington."

In 1819, on leave from his frigate of war, he was standing at the door of a small inn when a large coach and four drove up. On the high seat by the driver sat my grandfather McHutchinson and beside him his beautiful daughter, Elizabeth.

The moment Captain Sinclair set his eyes on her he gallantly came forward to assist her down. I expect she was nothing loathe to linger over the descent, leaning on the handsome young captain. As he later described it, "She seemed like an angel descending from heaven and I determined then and there to win her for my wife." Courteously assisting the old gentleman and introducing himself he was asked to join them at supper. From then on the affair went to a speedy and happy end. Elizabeth was nineteen and the captain twenty-nine. A dainty bride she must have been; it was told that her husband could span her waist with the thumb and forefinger of his two hands.

Living at first in the outskirts of Edinburgh, Captain Sinclair felt uneasy at leaving his wife and small son, George, so far from neighbors, especially after an experience she had with a stout country yokel evidently bent on thieving. In those days every door had a latch-chain, and on opening the door this chain was slipped over a hook leaving a small guarded slit through which one could see who was at the entrance. One day when the captain was away, hearing a knock at the door, my grandmother opened it but forgot to slip on the chain. Immediately a great burly man stuck his foot through the slightly opened door and began to press it open. With great presence of mind she turned her head towards the stair and called "Francis" in a loud voice. The man quickly withdrew his foot and she put on the chain and finally closed the door. The rogue disappeared, evidently afraid that "Francis" might get hold of him should he attempt to force his way in a second time.

The desk which the Duke of Wellington had given to Captain Sinclair had been prized for all these years, and on his resignation from the navy after his marriage, he used it constantly on his many journeys to and from London on Government business for the Inland Revenue Office. On returning from one of these trips he put up at one of the inns on the Post Road. The group of men gathered round the fire after supper admired the desk, whereupon Captain Sinclair told them its story. Next morning when ready for the coach he missed the desk, and though he hunted high and low and offered a large reward, nothing was ever seen or heard of it again. As a child I would dream of finding it in some old curiosity shop.

Shortly, the family moved to Stirling where they lived in a house called Bothwell Hall. It was situated near the wall of Stirling Castle, and there five other children were born, making a group of six sturdy, happy children: George, Jean, Helen, James, Francis and Anne the youngest, born on March 7, 1839. Bothwell Hall, as it is still called, was so near the wall surrounding the castle that the children would jump out of the second story window and play on the "Castle Walk." It was told of Jean that she got a very severe scolding for jumping across to the walk with 6-month-old Anne in her arms.

When I visited Scotland with my husband, Harry, and my two oldest children, Mary and Herman, in 1901, we went to Stirling to see my mother Anne's birthplace. We found it in good repair then and were allowed to go over the house where, from the upstairs window, I could vision the Sinclair children playing on the castle walk.

During these years, although Captain Sinclair was very much absorbed in business, he found time for social service work. The crying need was for reform in the liquor laws, and he was an eloquent speaker on temperance. His eldest son, George, was also gifted in this way, for it is recorded that late one afternoon his mother heard shouts, and on looking out saw her son, then only fifteen years old, being carried shoulder high by an enthusiastic crowd of men, who called out, "Take him to his mother and let her be proud of him."

Even though life seems to have been happy and prosperous there in Stirling, Captain and Mrs. Sinclair were seriously considering a tremendous change of scene. Wonderful reports of the opportuniteis in New Zealand were being brought back to the old country, so in October of 1839, with a number of other Scotch and English families, they decided to go to the new country. New Zealand was rapidly being opened up as an English colony and was finally declared such by the British Government early in 1840. George, the eldest son, was then nineteen years old, Jean about sixteen and James fifteen years old. The second daughter, Helen, was thirteen; Francis was six years old, while Baby Anne was only seven months old. Even in this modern age it would be an undertaking to break up one's home and move a family of eight persons, one an infant in arms, from Scotland to New Zealand. One is filled with admiration for the courageous woman who, without the least hesitation or regret, in fact with joy and happiness in the adventure as long as she could be with her beloved husband and children, started out from Stirling to Glasgow and from there in the big sailing vessel to the new land beyond the seas. The four-month voyage round the Cape of Good Hope and past Australia and Van Diemen's Land, as Tasmania was then called, was evidently a hard experience.

Grandmama suffered so terribly with seasickness that finally she lay in bed most of the time, causing the ship's captain much concern over "Mistress Sinclair's" health. She declared that once her foot touched land she would be quite restored. A few days after they landed in February, 1840 in Wellington, N. Z., she walked down to the landing and asked for the captain. He was amazed to see her looking well and quite recovered. The two maids had been perfectly well, also all the children during the long voyage, and little Anne learned to walk on the ship.

Before leaving Scotland, Captain Sinclair had purchased land to be chosen in the North Island after his arrival in New Zealand. Unfortunately the Government had not been able to secure the land from the Maoris, who were very fierce and wild in the North Island. Consequently much time was taken up waiting for arrangements.

The Sinclairs were all charmed with Wellington, a simple, quite settled community. One story told me by my mother shows how near the Maoris lived, and how thoughtful and wise my grandmother was in dealing with them. After such a long voyage there was a tremendous amount of laundry to be done. The two maids had been hard at work and had hung almost all the linen on the lines, where it was rapidly drying in the summer sunshine. During the afternoon a band of young Maoris from the nearby *Pa* (a Maori village) carried away every bit of clothing. Alfred Wallace, one of the young men who had accompanied the Sinclairs out from Scotland, prepared to run after them, first coming in to get his gun. Grandmama stopped him at once saying it would perhaps lead to an uprising on the part of the Maoris, and urged him to wait until Captain Sinclair returned. That evening on being told the story he commended her foresight, and next day when he went down to the *Pa* to see the chief (with whom the captain had already become acquainted) he was received with evident friendliness.

When the chief was told of what had happened he sent at once for the young marauders, ordering them to return every garment they had carried off the previous day. Then the old chief drawing his flax garments and blanket around him, and with a pigeon feather stuck through the roll of hair on the top of his head, stepped out of his beautifully carved *wharré* (house) and signalled to Captain Sinclair he would accompany him. With great dignity he led the way and when everything had been returned, he took his huge spear, inlaid with abalone shell, and stuck it down in the ground at the front door. "This," he said, "shows my friendship for you. No one will molest you and your family while you stay here." The spear remained in front of their door until they left Wellington in 1843.

After several exploring trips Captain Sinclair decided to take his family and party in three large boats to see the land he thought of buying. They took a tent with them and camped on the shore every night. My mother must have been then about three and a half years old for she had vivid memories of much that happened. Especially did she remember her father reading the Bible to them every evening and singing a hymn. All her life when she heard that grand old hymn "Dundee," her memories would flash back to this very trip down the beautiful shores of New Zealand with its innumerable bays and inlets. She would think of her father and hear him singing, "Oh God of Bethel by whose Hand Thy Children still are fed." As it was untrod country Captain Sinclair was alert to protect his family and party. A born leader, he seemed to have a sixth sense to warn him of any danger whether great or small. One night when all were asleep he heard, almost in his dreams, a strange cry which was unfamiliar. Rising at once to investigate he realized the cry was a call, the Maori call of *"Cooee."* The hour was about four A. M. and on a distant hill outlined against the dawn-lit sky he saw a Maori woman waving her arms and giving that peculiar call to which only a Maori could give volume that could be heard for miles. The extraordinary behavior of the woman made the captain suspicious. He wakened the family and the men sleeping under the upturned boats. With a rapidity born of apprehension all was packed up, the boats were launched and were putting out into the deep water when over the distant hill came literally a torrent of Maori men and women. All of them carried spears and clubs, and though they made friendly gestures when they reached the shore and called *"Heremai,"* Captain Sinclair felt they were not to be trusted after such a warlike demonstration. So waving a farewell to them and signalling that he must go on, he commanded the boatmen to pull down the bay.

This, and other experiences as well as rumors of the unfriendly attitude of the tribes in that vicinity, made him decide against remaining and settling there. Returning to Wellington he made an exchange and bought land in Pigeon Bay near Akaroa, Canterbury, on the South Island. For the voyage down the coast to the new property, Captain Sinclair bought a little sailing vessel called the *Richmond*.

A story that he had built the ship while in Wellington is without confirmation in the family history. The tale is not without interest, however, and the quotation goes as follows: "He had no bellows, no nails and had to hew the timber out of the bush. He must have been a resourceful man for the boat was finished within the year, ready for the trip South. His bellows was a cow's bladder attached to a musket-barrel. He made nails out of coopers' iron. Nothing seemed to daunt Captain Sinclair." With the last sentence everyone who knew him would heartily agree.

With Ebenezer Hay, a Scotchman and his family, the Sinclair Clan sailed down to Akaroa and on to Pigeon Bay in April, 1843. This sturdy Scotchman and his wife were a great help in settling on the new property. For the first months the two families lived in tents, then the *Richmond* was sold for ten cows valued at 20 pounds per head. These cows were in Akaroa and, to bring them over to Pigeon Bay, a trail had to be cut through the bush. This was done on a line of the path used by the Maoris. It took eight men three weeks to make this trail wide enough to bring the cattle over as the old path used by the Maoris was difficult to find except by an experienced bushman. The Maoris, like all primitive people, could find their way even though the track was only marked here and there by perhaps a broken twig or slight mark on a tree trunk.

Captain Sinclair had won the confidence of the Maoris almost immediately and with their help was able to do much. While the road over the hills to Akaroa was being engineered he had other men felling trees and sawing trunks into lumber. By July, 1843, a rough shack was built. Into this the Sinclairs moved and a year later, farther down the the Bay, a lovely house of white pine with red *totara* shingles was built, all cut from the forest by hand and under Captain Sinclair's supervision. I remember seeing a sketch of this new home which was most livable and attractive. It was named "*Craigforth*" after an estate in Scotland which they had often visited. Except for the Hay family, there were no neighbors other than Maoris.

The forest came down at intervals to the water's edge and a lovely stream supplied all the water for the house and garden. In this primeval forest were huge *kauri* trees as well as the white pine and *totara* trees. Also the *karaka* with its queer yellow berries which the Maoris buried for several weeks before eating. The *manuka* with its pretty pale pink starry blossoms, the *fuschia* whose berries were good to eat, and with which Anne later fed the birds. After climbing a tree and feeding the fledglings, she would mischievously enjoy watching the mother bird's anxiety when she found her babies so full of food that they would not respond to her call.

My mother always declared that only those who had seen that wonderful virgin forest in those early years could form any conception of its beauty. The lovely *kowhai* similar to our Hawaiian *ohai;* the *ngnaio*, our *naio;* and the numbers of ferns were also mentioned in my mother's stories from which I quote: "It was one of the most wonderful countries for wild birds. The woods were full of them, beautiful bright colored ones, and songsters, some equal to the English nightingale. One of these, the *tui*, was called the bell bird. He began his song early in the morning, one note after another falling clearly like a bell. When it was still dark and you heard that deep musical note, you knew that dawn was breaking in the east, and then all the birds would break into a great rush of song. The other birds too were a joy to us, the blackbirds, the tiny robins, the bright green parakeets, and of course the numbers of native pigeons for which the bay was named. The Maoris used an ingenious way of trapping the pigeons with a very sticky substance from the wild gum tree. This was spread on the ground and berries or grains sprinkled near. When the pigeons were caught in the gum, the Maoris who were hiding behind bushes near by, would leap out and kill them with long sticks.

"It was always a happy day in my life when the Maoris passed our place, travelling one way or the other. Often a hundred of them at a time, with their baskets and children and decoy birds, would camp for the night down on our shore, passing on next day to the reservation where they belonged. The Government had already set aside their *Pa* (Maori villages) as reservations where their homes would not be disturbed. When they camped near us, we always went down to see them. Each one carried a decoy, a beautiful little parrot, called in the native tongue a *kaka*, chained to a stick with a cross-piece at the top and pointed at the other end so that it could be pushed easily into the ground. When the Maoris wanted to get birds they took the decoys into a thick piece of woods and set them up on the sticks. The wild birds would come flying down, so that they could be easily killed with long sharp spears. These decoys were used entirely in hunting, as the Maoris had no guns until given them by the white men. The *kakas* were fed on seeds, nuts, berries, and potatoes. Potatoes had been given to the natives by the first white people to come to New Zealand, and there were great fields of them. They also grew wheat and all sorts of vegetables.

"There was a small *Pa* opposite us across the large bay, and in the potato season the natives vied with one another to sell us their produce. The first ones to paddle across would lay down their flax baskets in rows touching each other, and filled with the finest potatoes. My mother would come out and stretch a piece of cloth, probably enough for a dress, over the baskets and this would be the price for the potatoes. Those Maoris who did not get there in time would wait for a ship and sell to the captain, for some trifle, and the potatoes would be shipped to Australia, which was more populous than New Zealand. The natives were wise enough not to sell all their produce, but stored some away for the winter. They built store-houses high up on large heavy posts into which they chopped deep notches so that the rats could not climb up. Flax rope ladders were used to put the potatoes up into the store-houses, after which the ladders would be taken down. These store-houses were always a feature of the Maori villages.

"The shores of the bay were rocky and beautiful, and on the rocks one could find oysters, mussels, and exquisite shells. A favorite enjoyment and a common performance with us was to put up a bread-and-butter lunch, with plenty of salt, pepper and vinegar, take our oyster knives, and fly off to the beach. There we would sit on the rocks eating oysters and sandwiches. We also had all the fish we wanted with very little trouble. We had all kinds of boats to use in our bay from large sailing boats to little dinghys, and we grew to be very expert in managing them. I remember that my youngest brother, who was five years older than I, was quite a boatmen before he was seven years old. Even when we were in Wellington when I was only two or three years old, my mother would take me and go down the river with only this brother to manage the canoe, and she considered herself perfectly safe. As there were no bridges the only way we could cross the river was in boats or canoes. We always preferred the canoes, and were so at home in them that we could manage as well as the Maoris."

At times a whaler would sail into port and Mrs. Sinclair and Mrs. Hay would make purchases for the needs of their families, but after the road over the hills was made no one thought it any hardship to walk the fifteen miles to Akaroa to see the shops. Grandmama Sinclair would often go, as she was very fond of walking. In going to Akaroa she would be accompanied by her eldest son, George, just twenty years her junior. Before she became well known, the shop keepers would speak of her to George as "your sister." She was then forty-two years old! With all her family of six children as well as the hardships of the pioneer life she was still young, her hair untouched by grey, her eyes bright and sparkling, and no one could believe she was the mother of the tall young man of twenty-two.

The years closely following their settling in Pigeon Bay were full and busy ones. Captain Sinclair planned well, buying sheep and cattle, planting and harvesting. Sailing ships brought seeds and grains, potatoes grew luxuriantly. The Maoris were friendly and helpful, and prosperous years followed to 1846 when Captain Sinclair decided to go to Wellington to make further purchase of land adjoining his estate. He embarked on a little schooner taking his eldest son, George, and Alfred Wallace, who was supposed to be engaged to Jean, the oldest daughter, then about 18 years of age. The day they were to sail Grandmama Sinclair begged to be told when she might expect them to return. When Captain Sinclair replied, "In about three weeks," she exclaimed, "Three weeks! Oh Francis, I cannot bear to be without you as long as that." Anne, then seven years old, heard them speaking, and saw her father draw her mother back into the room for a farewell kiss. She wondered then how long "three weeks" really was. Little did they dream that they would never see or even hear of him again!

About the time the voyagers were expected, another vessel arrived in the bay. The master came on shore asking for Captain Sinclair. When told of the latter's departure on a certain schooner for Wellington three weeks earlier, the man exclaimed: "Why! I left Wellington less than a week ago and that boat had not arrived." Grandmama became alarmed at once; she sent messages to Sir George Grey, the governor, who was a close friend, also to the great Bishop Selwyn, and, with characteristic decision, immediately engaged the master of this schooner to sail up and down the coast on a search.

Sir George Grey came at once and Bishop Selwyn and friends from Akaroa, and every possible clue was investigated. Days lengthened into weeks, weeks to months, and finally all hope was abandoned. No trace, not even a spar, or sail, or evidence of any kind was ever found of the ship or of Captain Sinclair and the men who were with him. Desolate indeed was poor Grandmama Sinclair, left a widow at only 46. She was stunned and helpless in the face of this cruel loss of both husband and son. However, as her friends rallied round her, and the memory of what her husband had planned and wished for his children stirred her courage, her indomitable spirit came to her rescue.

With James, the second son, to help her and with constant visits and advice from Sir George Grey, she carried on the home and the estate and was comforted by the sympathy of everyone. Sir George Grey declared, "Captain Sinclair's death was the greatest loss not only to his family but to the whole colony of New Zealand."

CHAPTER II

The Life at Craigforth
1846–1863

AFTER the first two years of adjustment to the heartbreaking loss of her husband and son, Grandmama Sinclair became again the mainspring of her young family, who were noted for their charm and popularity. The governor, Sir George Grey, continued his affectionate interest and was able to arrange her business affairs advantageously, although she had to go to Wellington, where she spent two years in connection with the settlement of her husband's estate.

Among the family friends were many whose names were foremost in making the early history of New Zealand: The Cholmondeleys; Bishop and Mrs. Harper and their girls and boys; Henry Gladstone, cousin of the great William Gladstone; Dr. and Mrs. Moore who lived near Lyttelton; Sir Willaim Fox, who painted beautifully in water colors, and Lady Fox; a Mr. Campbell and his pretty daughter Blanche; the Carringtons and the Aylmers, whose daughter, Kate, was one of Anne's most intimate friends. Kate Aylmer later married a Mr. Rattray and went to live in Dunedin. All these, and many more, were friends of the Sinclair family. A tutor for Frank, and later a governess for Anne, brought a closer touch with literature and the fine arts.

The house "Craigforth" built with such care by Captain Sinclair, became a center of lively happy times with three lovely girls and two handsome boys. The garden was full of flowers, the walks lined with beds of daisies, violets,

Craigforth
Pigeon Bay, Banks Peninsula, New Zealand
Painting by Chevalier 1866

fuschias, in fact every flower brought from the old country, all of which grew luxuriantly for the mere planting. The veranda was covered with Banksia roses and it was Anne's special duty, and greatest delight, to prune and care for these roses. I can remember her telling of the admiration of visitors for the garden, and her pleasure in their praise.

Frank was five years older, but having no boy near his age made a tremendous chum of his sister whom he always called "Bob" even in their later years. She became so wiry and strong with that splendid out-door life that she was always able to share in all his activities. She could mend a sail, caulk a boat, clean a gun, mend shoes, in fact she could do anything, and yet in her grownup years was beautiful, dainty, and feminine. Fishing, boating, tramping, hunting, all of these she revelled and excelled in.

When unexpected guests would arrive Anne would run out into the forest with her fowling-piece, and bring home half a dozen wild pigeons. New Zealand pigeons are about the size of a three months old chicken, and very tender and tasty. Grandmama Sinclair was evidently a good cook for people raved over the delicious birds she would roast for them.

Accidents happened of course, but fortunately nothing very serious, though when Anne was quite young she had a narrow escape from disfigurement for life. Frank evidently was playing with gunpowder, making it flare up in the pan. Without warning Anne to be careful, he let her touch the match. So quickly did it flare up that her face was seriously burned; eyebrows and eyelashes and hair as far back as her close-fitting sunbonnet would allow, were all singed off! She ran quickly home and Grandmama Sinclair at once covered her face with olive oil (a precious bottle she had just bought from the French captain) and cotton, and kept her in bed for days. Fortunately, though she suffered much at first, she never had the slightest scar. My mother declared it was the quiet care and nursing. In the old days, especially in Scotch families, great stress was put on *"rest and careful feeding*" when ill or after any accident. Belief that nature would cure if given a chance, made all Scotch mothers careful in keeping a child in bed, and fed with a very light diet.

One day Anne was playing with a little girl who was visiting at Craigforth. She suggested playing at fishing with real hooks and lines which was against the rule, and soon showed her lack of knowledge of how to fish by throwing her hook and line towards Anne. The hook caught in the latter's lower lip and then, without listening to Anne who wanted to run home for help, Maisie jerked the hook out, tearing the flesh on the inside of the lip most cruelly.

Frightened then at the results of her carelessness, she ran beside Anne on the way back to the house, threatening her with all sorts of dire things if the grown-ups were told the truth. Anne loyally took the blame of the accident, but next day, after the visitors had left, she told her mother what had really happened. Grandmama's only remark was: "Well, I am glad you told me, for I could not believe *you* would have done anything so foolish."

Everyone walked or sailed; no mention of horses or horseback rides was made till later years after they were grown-up, when they would have riding parties with their young friends in Akaroa. Anne became an expert rider and sat her side saddle perfectly.

The evenings at Craigforth were spent in reading aloud or music. *No* cards were ever seen in the Sinclair home as they were *absolutely* disapproved of by Grandmama. The boys James (Hamie) and Francis (Frank) took turns in reading aloud as their mother and sisters sewed. No sewing machines were invented then or even dreamed of. All house and bed linen, underwear, dresses and men's clothing (except the heavy suits which were sent out from England) were made by the girls and grandmama by hand. In the happy quiet reading hours they became thoroughly acquainted with all of Shakespeare, Thackeray, Dickens and other literature of the day—Byron's poems, Sir Walter Scott, Sir Thomas Moore's poems, and of course their own

Scotch poet, Robert Burns. They shared the excitement of the times when Dickens first brought out his wonderful novels.

Anne had tremendous dramatic ability which her life had accentuated, and the people of Shakespeare's plays, and the characters of Dickens' and Thackery's novels became living personalities to her. She was naturally talented, had a lovely contralto voice which blended sweetly with Helen's soprano. Grandmama Sinclair had bought a little piano on which Anne quickly learned to play after a few lessons from her governess, Mrs. Beechy. She could sketch fairly well in water colors as well as with pencil, and later, when Sir William and Lady Fox visited at Craigforth, Anne had many a lesson from Sir William.

It was very much the fashion to write games on words, and limericks and these were often the amusement of the evening. One I can remember hearing of was by Aunt Helen. The words given her were "tongs", "wrongs", "fender", "tender", and she wrote out the following:

> When I stir up the fire with the tongs
> I think upon all my wrongs,
> But when I sit with my feet on the fender
> My heart grows uncommonly tender.

One evening Grandmama came in and Anne begged her to write an acrostic at which they were all trying their hands. Grandmama sat down and wrote quickly the following to "Annie" which the latter treasured all her life.

> Accept, dear Annie, a mother's love,
> No love so pure this earth can boast,
> No serpent's wiles its strength can move
> In Paradise when all was lost
> Eve saved this ray, how great the cost.

Naturally there were romances in the lives of these young people. Jean, the eldest daughter, was a dear, unselfish, helpful personality. In 1848 she married Captain Thomas Gay, a widower with one son about five years old. This boy lived with his Aunt in Hobart Town, and did not enter into the Sinclair lives until later years.

Captain Gay owned a fine sailing vessel of the British Merchant Marine, on which he took his bride on a honeymoon voyage to Australia and Van Diemen's Land. Later she often accompanied him on his ship as he plied between New Zealand and Australia. As children we loved the story of the little kangaroo pet which Captain Gay brought to his children from there. It soon grew too large for the children to play with, however, and a pen was built for it. One night it escaped into the forest and was never caught though often seen leaping rapidly away through the bush. After many years it turned quite white and was dubbed "old man kangaroo." Finally, my mother said, they lost track of him and supposed he had died a lonely death after living a most lonely life.

Captain Gay built a house for Jean about half a mile down the bay. Here Anne found an outlet for her energies, as she was often called upon to stay with Jean when Captain Gay was away. Their eldest son, named George, was born in 1849, ten years younger than his Aunt Anne. She evidently was a great factor in the lives of the Gay children of whom there were six—George, Annie (who died at the age of two), Francis, Eliza, Charles, and Alice, born in Hawaii after they left New Zealand.

Helen, the second of the Sinclair daughters, was supposed to be delicate, and was always waited on hand and foot by Anne. Being so much older Helen dominated her, especially as Anne, besides being aboundingly healthy, was of a sunny helpful disposition. Helen too was the prettiest, and always had the pick of anything that came to the house in the way of things to wear, and evidently the whole family worshipped her. She was very clever, and as children we all thought she was the perfect hostess, in fact, quite the *grande dame* in looks and manner.

In 1850 she married Charles Barrington Robinson and went to live at Akaroa where he had much property. He was twenty years Helen's senior, a clever man of 42. He had been chief magistrate in 1840 for the Southern part of New Zealand, under appointment by Governor Hobson, the first governor of New Zealand, and founder of the city of Auckland. It is recorded that he was sent out in *H.M.S. Brittomart* and did splendid service for the colony in establishing British authority at each port of call. In this way Mr. Robinson frustrated the intentions of the French who had sent Captain L'Anglois out with a load of 65 emigrants in an old war ship which, with officers and crew, made a total of 105 souls.

Another armed ship *"L'Aube"* in command of Captain Lavaud, preceded them so as to be ready to protect the emigrants. Before *L'Aube's* arrival however Mr. Robinson had erected a pole and hoisted the Union Jack in His Britannic Majesty's name on Green Point, when the French ships came to port in Akaroa Bay.

Mr. Robinson was especially fitted for the position of chief magistrate, being a remarkably clever lawyer and a good linguist. His knowledge of the French language enabled him to give great assistance to the emigrants and other settlers in their business and local affairs. The governor allowed the Frenchmen to arrange with Mr. Robinson, through Captain Lavaud, to administer French law amongst them. This Captain Lavaud was a genial and charming man, and became very friendly with the Sinclairs. He was especially nice to the younger ones, often inviting Annie and Frank over to the Block House where he lived, and giving them presents from the French stores laid in there.

After Mr. Robinson resigned the position of chief magistrate, he returned to England, and a Mr. John Watson succeeded him as "Resident Magistrate" which title he retained for many years. He and Mrs. Watson were close friends of the Sinclairs.

Mr. Robinson, after his return from England and marriage to Helen, devoted himself to his property and home in Akaroa. He made a specialty of importing fine cattle and is said to have brought the first short-horn cattle from England. He also brought birds of all kinds, among these a pair of English pheasants which he gave to Grandmama. They soon multiplied all over the peninsula, vieing with the native pigeons in numbers.

When little Aubrey Robinson was one year old, Helen appeared one forenoon at her mother's house, having walked all the way from Akaroa carrying the child. She announced that she had left her husband and had come home to stay. Mr. Robinson came at once after his wife, and had long interviews with Grandmama, but all to no avail. Helen would not even see him, nor let the little boy be taken from her, and no one seemed to know the reason for this absolute estrangement, or what the real trouble was. Mr. Robinson then returned to England, only coming back about 1864 after the Sinclair family had left Craigforth, to dispose of his property.

Frank had a romantic nature and when about 23 years old was very desperately in love with the beautiful Blanche Campbell who lived with her father in Akaroa. She shared his love and the match evidently met with the approval of both families, and Anne, then about 18, was devoted to her sister-to-be. Some estrangement however took place, no one could discover what it was. At this time Frank began his writing, and many of his poems were published in the Akaroa *Times*.

Tennyson was the favorite poet of the day, the late "fifties" and early "sixties," and possibly influenced Frank to some extent as his earlier work shows a distinct leaning to the Tennysonian style. Anne was very sympathetic in these literary ventures of this beloved brother. With him she shared her love of the best, and also wrote stories and poetry, while she memorized easily everything she liked. This gift was a joy to her children and one which unfortunately none of them inherited. In much later years I can remember her reciting the whole of Byron's beautiful poem beginning, "The castled crag of Drachenfels frowns oe'r the wide and winding Rhine," while we were all sailing down that beautiful river in 1884.

James was, as my mother declared, the finest character of them all; everyone loved him and sought his advice. He was quiet but very affectionate and interested and happy in helping everyone. Clever and well read, he was a walking encyclopedia, as he was a tremendous student and his remarkable memory retained a vivid knowledge of every subject. In fact when any question came up about political, religious, or historical subjects, his family or friends would exclaim, "Let's ask Hamie about it."

No stories of him or of any love affairs ever came to my knowledge. He was, like Grandmama, contented and happy in letting the others have their way. Though Anne had many suitors—Arthur Aylmer, one of the fine young Harper men, a Mr. Gillispie, young Mr. Gladstone and others—she was not to be won. Romance had touched her from a different quarter. James Montgomery of Dunedin had visited at Craigforth when coming up the coast on business; and though he was very attentive, he never said anything to her, and she in her busy happy life only thought of him as a romantic possibility.

About 1862 Frank and Helen, both of whom were restless and unhappy, began to urge a departure of the family for wider fields and opportunities. The land which Captain Sinclair had set out to buy on his last disastrous voyage had never been purchased by Mrs. Sinclair. The estate was too circumscribed for this growing family, and, they argued, the younger generation should be better provided for in the future. Perhaps it was only the adventurous spirit of the times, but even so Anne and James did not want to leave Craigforth and New Zealand. However, the others carried the day and persuaded Grandmama to sell the estate at Pigeon Bay and go to British Columbia or California, from where stories of the huge ranchos of the Spanish Dons and their descendants had fired Frank's imagination. The beautiful home and estate had a quick sale, a Mr. Holmes buying it and allowing them time to make their preparations for the long voyage. Their friends all over New Zealand were astounded when the news of the sale was published. All were dismayed and many broken hearted at this decision. In those days news travelled more slowly and also this plan had characteristically been kept more or less secret, so that to many of even their most intimate friends, it came as a bombshell, especially to James Montgomery. He left everything at once for the several days' journey to Akaroa, and to Craigforth, and going straight to Anne in the garden, he begged her to become his wife and remain in New Zealand. He told her of his deep love from their very first meeting, and that he had only restrained himself from speaking to her on account of getting himself into a better financial position to marry. She did not give him an answer for he came several times, and though she was still romantic about him, and spoke to me long years after of him as her first love, she was influenced by her family. Hamie alone was sympathetic, the others, especially Frank and Helen, making a terrible campaign against him. They declared he was dastardly in waiting till they had sold the estate, in fact made him out to be quite a villain, and she, who was so devoted to her family, felt they must be right and refused him. He left no stone unturned, and many were the love letters sent after her, imploring her to accept him. Even after they had been gone a year or more he wrote he would give up everything to live with her wherever she wished. My mother told me all this when we heard of James Montgomery asking for news of her from a young friend of ours when they met on the *S.S. Zealandia* en route to New Zealand. Also again after my own marriage she told me the story. Later after her death and Mr. Montgomery's, we entertained the son, James Montgomery, Jr., who, however, had never heard of his father's early romance, but was intensely interested.

To go back to the departure of the Sinclairs from Craigforth, a barque of 300 tons was bought, named *Bessie*, which was fitted up with extra comforts for the family. All sorts of supplies were put on board—a cow and hay and grain for her, chickens, fine merino sheep, jams and jellies made at home, quantities of apples from the orchard, also books, clothing and all the paraphernalia of a home, even to a piano.

When all was in readiness and the sale of the estate concluded, a story went around that all their money in Spanish gold was stored in chests in the hold of the ship. I never could get this legend corroborated, as I only heard of it in Honolulu after my mother's death, but anyway I *do* know that it was not Spanish gold but good solid British sovereigns literally "worth their weight in gold!"

It is quite probable that the Sinclairs had a draft or letter of credit. Somehow though, *I* feel the story of the chests in the hold of the *Bessie* is true. It fits in with those adventurous days, and with the way the Sinclairs quietly managed all their affairs.

Finally one April morning in 1863, early autumn in New Zealand, they fared forth in the barque *Bessie* with all sails set and Grandmama Sinclair's heart did not quail. Even as twenty-four years before she had set out from Scotland on unknown seas, and founded a home, so did she start again when sixty-three years old, doubting not but that they would find what they were seeking, the El Dorado of their dreams.

CHAPTER III

The Voyage of the Bessie

APRIL 1863 TO SEPTEMBER 1863

IN A FEW DAYS they were quite at home on the *Bessie* and the clan enjoyed the adventure. On board were my grandmother, Mrs. Elizabeth Sinclair; Captain and Mrs. Thomas Gay and their children, George, Francis, Eliza and Charles (the latter not quite two years old), and James, Captain Gay's son by his first marriage; Mrs. Charles Barrington Robinson and her son Aubrey; and James, Frank and Anne Sinclair, the unmarried children of Mrs. Sinclair, besides several servants and the crew. Evidently Captain Gay had made a good choice when he purchased the barque for she sailed over the ocean without too much rolling. Captain Gay was an expert in handling his craft and as time was of no immediate consequence he would change the course when it became too rough, and run with the wind for a while to rest the voyagers from the rolling and pitching. Grandmama too was very comfortable and enjoyed the whole trip.

One of my favorite stories of the voyage, and my mother gave it full dramatic effect in the telling, was of a calm day, as the whole family was sitting on the deck. Suddenly they saw the tentacles of a huge octopus coming up over the side of the vessel, grasping the mast and rigging. The ship listed to one side with the weight of the terrifying monster as its head and body came in sight over the rail. Everyone was frozen with terror, as one of its long tentacles could easily have been flung around them, dragging them to its beak-like mouth. After peering around with its uncanny eyes, for a few minutes, it loosed its hold and slid back into the ocean. Captain Gay asserted that after this experience he could confirm the stories told by whalers and sailors of finding huge pieces of octopus as large as a man's thigh in the bellies of sharks, as these tentacles were certainly as large as that near the body of the monster and they tapered up fifteen or twenty feet as they stretched up the rigging.

Their first port was at Tahiti where they were entranced by the beauty of the lagoons, the exquisite fronds of pink coral to be seen through the translucent water, the palms and tropical foliage, the high peaks reaching up to the clouds and the deep valleys through which tumbled beautiful rivers and waterfalls. It all seemed a fairyland and they enjoyed several weeks meeting the British Consul and other pleasant people. The consul gave a picnic and horseback ride up to one of the high mountains for them. While returning through the tropic scenery, he proposed to Anne saying he had fallen in love with her at first sight. Anne however, whose heart had been left in New Zealand, was not to be won by this new swain even though so charming. As a parting gift he gave her a lovely specimen of the pink coral, which Captain Gay in some way slung at the stern of the vessel out of reach of the waves.

"One day in Tahiti," my mother wrote, "we sailed a long way along the coral reefs and landed with our lunch baskets to picnic near a native village. A tall fine looking native met us, clad only in a *malo* (loin cloth), and asked in French what he could do for us. When we told him we were travellers he asked the privilege of making a native feast for us. He set to work with his helpers and cooked a meal in the native ovens, which are underground, meanwhile telling us the history of the place, and that he was a Roman Catholic missionary. After an hour and a half he seated us on the ground in proper Tahitian fashion, then said he must run back to his house and dress. In a few minutes he came back with a clean white European shirt on, and nothing else! but as it came down to his knees he was extremely well dressed.

He took his place at the head of the table, pronounced a long blessing, and served us a delicious meal.

Another incident in Tahiti amused us very much. My sister, Helen, and I dropped into a French store to look at the Parisian things displayed. The salesman was a small, dark complexioned man whom we supposed to be a Frenchman. We began at once to speak to him in our best French but he could not understand us. We were perplexed, as we had been told that we were good French scholars. Finally I was tired of the situation and said to my sister, 'There is no use talking any more as we can't understand each other.' The little 'Frenchman' clapped his hands together and leaned over the counter as he said with a strong Scotch accent, 'Losh, leddys, are ye Scotch?', and he began to weep. For some time we talked about Scotland, and the poor homesick little man thanked us profusely for our visit."

Sailing over the Pacific, they saw and passed several islands, and saw, on the horizon, the peaks of Mauna Loa and Mauna Kea on Hawaii.

It has been recorded by Miss Isabella Bird that they landed at Honolulu for a short time before going on to the Northwest, but in my mother's notes she only mentions seeing the mountains as they sailed by the Hawaiian group. She was then twenty-four years old and kept very clear impressions of their voyage all her life.

They arrived in Victoria in early June and at first were agreeably impressed with the island. The bay, the town, the English people, all were interesting and attractive, but after they made several expeditions to see the ranch or sheep farming lands, and realized the tremendous task to clear the forest, they were rather daunted. They were unfavorably impressed by the Canadian Indians, as well as the pest of mosquitoes which flew round their heads every time they ventured into the forest. The aborigines on Vancouver Island frightened them with their lower lips so repulsively turned out and held down with a sliver of white bone. They were so unlike the happy Maoris that a feeling of uneasiness was aroused in everyone. The fishing was fascinating and all were astonished at the rush of salmon at the mouth of the rivers. They would row over to the outlet of any stream and literally pick out of the water numbers of fish.

They met a number of people who were anxious to have them remain but a Mr. Henry Rhodes, connected with the Hudson Bay Co., was especially kind and advised them to go to the Sandwich Islands as the winter was coming on and the rains in California would make it difficult to take the long trips over the mesas to see the ranch lands there. In those days all travel was by horseback, covered wagon, or coach-and-four, and the roads in winter were well nigh impassable. Mr. Rhodes' advice struck them favorably and as he gave them a letter of introduction to his brother, Mr. Godfrey Rhodes, in Honolulu, they decided to sail for that port. These two gentlemen were brothers of Mrs. Thomas Brown, grandmother of Harry Martens von Holt—another interesting link in the two families. Before their departure, and with Anne's consent, Grandmama gave Mr. Rhodes the lovely pink coral, thinking they would find more in the Sandwich Islands. Off the coast near the mouth of the Columbia River, they experienced dreadful swells which frightened both children and grown-ups, though Captain Gay said he had heard it was a common occurrence in that part of the Pacific. After about two days in which Captain Gay never left the tiller, they got out of the swells and struck the trade winds, which brought them comfortably down to the Islands. They made the port of Honolulu on September 17, 1863, after a twenty-eight day voyage, as is chronicled in the "Friend" of October and in the Pacific Commercial Advertiser of September 24th of that year.

The Rev. Samuel Damon was Seaman chaplain, and it is recorded in Isabella Bird's book *Six Months in the Sandwich Islands*, that he told her the following story which I quote: "On going down to the wharf he was surprised to find the trim barque with its large family party on board, with a beautiful old lady at its head, books, pictures, work, even a piano, and all that could add refinement to a floating home, with cattle and sheep of valuable breeds in pens on the deck."

With Father Damon's help, they found a house to rent called "John Brown's house on the Plains" which I believe was between Punahou and "Little Britain" the house of Captain and Mrs. Luce, where now the Honolulu Dairymen's Association is situated on Sheridan Street. The first night on shore they were quite unprepared for mosquitoes and all had a restless night with the exception of Anne, who was weary after getting all the family settled, and was always a sound sleeper. Next morning the exposed half of her face was so bitten by mosquitoes that everyone thought she had broken out with measles. Her rosy cheek and clear complexion showed on the side which had been buried in her pillow, but no one could believe she had slept so soundly all night long.

They soon became acquainted with the people of Honolulu. Among them was Mr. Wyllie, who was Minister of Foreign Affairs, and at whose house, "Rosebank", Lady Franklin stayed when she visited Honolulu after the loss of her famous husband in the Northwest Passage had been confirmed. Mr. Wyllie had come to Honolulu in 1844 with General Miller and both were good friends of my father and mother. The Thomas Browns, Herman von Holts, Bishop and Mrs. Staley, Mr. and Mrs. Synge, the Judds, and other members of the community also extended a welcome to the Sinclairs.

A beautiful levee given by Mr. Wyllie in honor of King Kamehameha IV and Queen Emma was much enjoyed by the Sinclairs, and there they saw their first *Hula Kui* danced by none other than the king himself.

The missionaries had banned all hulas, and the Court adhered to that ruling, dancing instead the quadrilles, lancers and minuet, the more stately dances of our grandparents' time. The king, however, evidently enjoyed his prerogative of dancing the Spear Dance which told the story of his illustrious forebear, Kamehameha the Great, who stood before his warriors and warded off spears cast at him to test his skill and endurance.

I quote from my mother's notes: "Though the land in California was so cheap we knew that that country was not yet in a settled condition, while here in Hawaii we were at home in a pleasant life and a settled community. In looking about for ranches that would suit us, however, it was difficult to find what we wanted, as a law, 'The Great Mahele' had recently been passed by the Hawaiian Legislature enabling the natives to take up little holdings wherever they liked. Such numbers of these had been taken up all over the islands that it was well-nigh impossible to find a large enough tract of land for our purpose. These holdings are called *kuleanas* and though they broke up the large ranch lands, no reasonable person could object to this law, as it was a fine thing for the natives.

"After some months of looking, during which we were offered Kahuku on northern Oahu by Mr. Wyllie, Ford Island in Pearl Harbor, by Dr. Ford, and the adjoining lands of Honouliuli and Ewa, all of which could have been bought for a song and which James Campbell bought in 1877, we gave up and decided to leave for California. When King Kamehameha heard of this he told us that if we would stay in Hawaii he would sell us a whole island, having a population of about three hundred natives. After my brothers had investigated the place they were so enthusiastic that we accepted the King's offer, and for $10,000 we bought the island of Niihau off the coast of Kauai.

"It was at this time that we met Mr. Valdemar Knudsen whose estate was on Kauai, our nearest neighbor. He had been there several years and proved a most helpful friend, giving us needed advice and interpreting for us to the natives. Not a single one of the 300 men and women on Niihau, could speak a word of English, so we had always to take an interpreter with us until we learned to speak and read the language ourselves. As this was so imperative we soon became quite proficient. Being young and full of energy, I occupied myself by teaching young and old to speak English, to write a little, and to read the Bible.

"We had bought sheep and cattle from the big ranches on Hawaii, and took them, with some fine sheep we had brought with us from New Zealand, to begin our new ranch on Niihau, where we had to build houses and generally organize everything from the beginning.

"The Rev. Mr. Rowell who had charge of the Niihau Mission, lived at Waimea on Kauai, and made monthly visits to us. We became very good friends and helped him all we could. The usual way of crossing the channel was by large open whale boats, manned by native sailors, and many were the adventurous trips back and forth over the twenty-five or thirty miles between the islands. Occasionally a small sailing vessel could be chartered, but that was a most tedious trip as the winds were apt to be very light. I experienced more than once a three day trip over, so we naturally preferred the boat, which with all its discomforts, still got one over in from four to six hours time.

"During the building of the house we lived in the main village Puuwai. One day mother appealed to the chief as she had missed a teaspoon. He promised to help her find it, causing the family much amusement over the proceedings. First he lined all the children in the immediate neighborhood up in a row and told them he could see with his magic glass into their hearts, and would discover the culprit. The glass proved efficacious even though it was only a bit of looking glass he held up to his eye as he passed down the line. When he came near one small boy the little fellow began to tremble, and crying out in fear, produced the spoon from his torn pants pocket before the old chief had even reached him."

After the building of "The House" on a bluff near Nonopapa and the settling of the family, Captain Gay took the *Bessie* back to Honolulu and on south to Australia, there to sell the vessel. After consummating the sale in Sydney he unfortunately contracted pneumonia and died, never seeing

"The House"
Kiekie, Niihau–*Bishop Museum Photo*

his youngest child Alice, who was born on Niihau on March 17, 1865.

Soon the family realized how cut off they were from all educational advantages and wrote away for tutors, and a number came and went. Many friends visited, especially their nearest neighbor Valdemar Knudsen. He brought over young William Brigham who was a botanist collecting specimens of the island flora for the famous Harvard collection in Boston, and who was later head of the Bishop Museum in Honolulu.

During 1864 and '65 Frank and Anne went on with their reading and his writing—she too composing several poems of merit. She was always, even in after years, his final tribunal. If she liked it then it was good. Among the books written and published by Francis Sinclair are: *Ballads and Poems from the Pacific*, *Under North Star and Southern Cross*, and *From the Four Winds*. One evening when looking at the sunset over the little island of Kaula to the southwest of Niihau, she dared him to write a poem to the island. He accepted the challenge and they both went to their desks to meet an hour later to compare their work. When she read her verses he exclaimed, "You've won, I cannot do better than that." Sweet praise to her who admired and adored him!

"Kaula"
by Anne Sinclair

Far away upon the ocean
Where the tropic skies are bright,
Where the silvery billow breaketh
Over sands of golden light,
Stands an islet sad and lone.
There it dwells in lonely grandeur
Midst its corals and its flowers
With its caverns echoing loudly
When the tempest quickly lowers
And the angry surges roar.

> To the sea it told the secret
> Of its sad and lonely heart,
> And the ocean answered wildly
> "Thou and I can never part!
> We have borne the strife of ages,
> And together will we stand
> Through the tempest and the sunshine,
> Firmly clasping hand in hand,
> Heart to heart and soul to soul
> While the ages onward roll."

Anne's homesickness for Craigforth and New Zealand in those early Niihau days was very acute, and I recall her telling me of a dream which constantly repeated itself. In this dream she was about to round the point in her boat and see the old home of Craigforth, when she invariably waked weeping before she reached the scene. I can remember her say "Oh why could I not sleep on till I saw it once more, even if only in a dream."

Late in 1865 Frank announced his intention to go to New Zealand and marry his cousin Isabella McHutchison, who with her parents and family had come to Canterbury, N. Z., from Scotland several years before the Sinclairs had left Craigforth. This was a blow to Anne, as she had given up a love affair and left New Zealand mainly for Frank's sake. However she did all she could, on their return, for their happiness, and was as usual the mainspring of their lives on Niihau.

During these years many pleasant and interesting visitors came to Niihau. Several times a man-of-war anchored off the bay, and the captain and officers made the house their headquarters. Once an English family, Lord and Lady Brassy, cruising around the world in their yacht, touched there. They also enjoyed the British Commissioner who later brought his wife and daughter to visit. All enjoyed the pleasures of the island life, horseback riding, swimming, surfriding, and roaming the beautiful shores which were covered with exquisite sea shells. These were a never ceasing joy to Anne and she had a notable collection.

Mrs. Francis Sinclair and Family at Makaweli House
1893
Seated l to r: Francis Gay, Mrs. George Gay, Mrs. Sinclair,
Mrs. Charles Robinson, Mrs. Aubrey Robinson with Aylmer,
Aubrey Robinson and Sinclair
Standing l to r: Eliza Gay, Francis Sinclair,
Mrs. Francis Sinclair, J. H. Wodehouse
Bishop Museum Photo

When late in 1866 she told the family of her engagement to Valdemar Knudsen, Frank asked "Is it because I have married that you are leaving us?" To this question she laughingly replied, "Nonsense, Frank, you must realize I want a life companion and home of my own as much as you do." As Grandmama, Aunt Helen and Aunt Jean, with their six children, also the newlyweds, and James, were all living in the same house, it seems to our modern way of thinking almost unbelievable that they could all live happily together. All felt Anne was cruel to leave them and want her own home, though, as they thought highly of Valdemar Knudsen, they had no real reason for objecting to her marriage, and were glad of Anne's choice. Valdemar was very romantic over "his Annie," as he had never been in love before, though now forty-six years old. He wrote expressively showing his deep feeling, and his love of poetry and nature; his interest in collecting flora and fauna, his enthusiasm and love of adventure, all coincided with her feelings and brought a ready response from her. She always took the keenest interest in all his many and varied activities. I quote her acrostic written to him in 1866:

> *V*oice of Love, oh magic sound
> *A*ll the world with music filling,
> *L*ow it falls on listening ears
> *D*reams of bliss the heart is thrilling.
> *E*ver more shall sweet love brighten
> *M*orn and noon, and starry night
> *A*nd e'en sorrows burden lighten
> *R*esting in Love's gentle light.
>
> *K*indling all the earth with glory
> *N*eath the evening's peaceful ray
> *U*ttered was the mystic story
> *D*awn of Love's eternal day
> *S*tars burst forth in joyous singing,
> *E*very flower rich perfume flinging
> *N*ight her sweet Love anthems ringing.

Shortly after their engagement Anne, Helen, and James visited at "Waiawa" Valdemar later taking them to "Halemanu," the little mountain house. I recall my father telling me that Mrs. Smith of Koloa first named the place "Little Norway," but after my mother's marriage, she and my father renamed it "Halemanu," (House of the Birds) a most appropriate name, as Hawaiian birds of every description could be seen in the forest all around the cabin. The *oo*, black with a yellow feather under each wing, was under a royal taboo, as the yellow feathers were used for the royal cloaks and helmets. The red *iiwi* and *apapane*, the green birds, the *elepaio*, called *"Kahuna Kalaiwaa,"* and others too numerous to mention, filled the early mornings with their singing, a very lovely and happy memory to me. No one nowadays, not having seen the primeval mountain forest, can have any conception of the beauty and grandeur of it all. The Hawaiians were always most careful not to kill the birds. The ones whose yellow feathers were used were trapped with some sticky preparation, and after the feathers were taken the birds were released.

The little mountain home had been included in my father's lands when he bought the leases of the Kekaha, Poki, and Mana lands from Messrs. Archer and Gruben. Both my mother and father preferred Hawaiian names for places, the latter remarking that many names and much of the old lore would eventually disappear. His thoughts on the subject have been borne out, as it is now difficult to get a true picture of ancient Hawaiian life from the natives themselves. How fortunate that our missionaries and other clever men and women of those early days wrote such interesting details in their diaries and journals.

This congenial party of four already mentioned also rode over to visit Dr. and Mrs. Smith at Koloa, and went on to Lihue to visit the Rices, Isenbergs and Wilcoxes, Valdemar proudly showing off his charming fiancee. Mrs. Smith told me many years later that she would never forget the lovely Miss Sinclair as she rode in on a very spirited horse, clad in a long dark green riding habit with tightly buttoned waist, a green hat with curling grey ostrich plume, carrying a riding crop. Her gay, happy personality brought life to all the old families who had lived there so long and were of a quieter, perhaps more prim, upbringing than Anne's had been. Consequently they all fell in love with her and thought Knudsen a most fortunate man.

My mother and father were married on February 12, 1867, in the little Hawaiian church on Niihau by the dear old pastor. Her simple white dress and the fresh orange blossoms picked early in the morning by her devoted brother Frank only enhanced her charm and loveliness. After the ceremony and wedding breakfast they rode to Kii in the late afternoon, spending the night there and taking the whale boat early the next morning to "Waiawa," her new home and life to which she brought so much enthusiasm and romance.

* * * * *

One month after their marriage, accompanied by James and Helen, who joined them from Niihau, they started off on a trip to Europe which was to be so interesting and wonderful to Anne.

Anne writes: "We rode all the way to Lihue to board the little schooner which was to take us to Honolulu, where we enjoyed meeting our numerous friends again. Several weeks later we sailed for San Francisco and it was on this ship during a heavy fog and tremendous seas that I experienced one of my narrowest escapes. On the last night the wind died down, and the ship drifted nearer and nearer to the rocks off the Golden Gate. Most of the passengers were frantic with fear as all on deck watched our ship rolling toward those terrible breakers. Women were on their knees praying. I looked on for awhile, then said to my husband, 'This is not laying up any strength for our final struggle. I am going down to rest. When we must put on our life belts, come and tell me.' I put on some warm clothes, and lying down slept quietly until I was awakened by bright sunshine streaming into my cabin. Valdemar was sitting beside me looking at me with admiration, and told me a strong land breeze had sprung up as the ship was on the verge of plunging into the breakers and we were safely out beyond the Farralones. When I went to breakfast, I would not have known the captain, as he looked broken and aged, and white as a sheet. When I spoke to him he said, 'Mrs. Knudsen, if everyone had left me alone last night as you did, I would be a different man this morning.'

"We spent a few days in San Francisco and then went on to Panama. One little incident occurred on the way down showing the lawlessness of that coast. We stopped at Acapulco and went ashore in small boats manned by Mexicans. The beautiful little bay is surrounded by mountains and, when one is inside, the entrance is hidden from view. We wandered around the quaint little city until it was late and dark when we returned to take the boats. As we came up to the ship my brother helped my sister and myself on board, leaving Valdemar to pay the boatmen. After ten minutes or so we looked around for him. My brother had not seen him, and the vessel was about to leave. I rushed to the captain, telling him I feared my husband had been abducted by the boatmen and asking him not to leave without his passenger. The captain ordered boats lowered and the gangplank put down again. While the captain was preparing to go on shore to report his being lost, Valdemar suddenly appeared. He told us that the boatmen had kept him talking until he was alone, then quickly pushed the boat off and pulled rapidly into the darkness. Though he called, he was not heard and they took all his money, which, as he was the purse bearer of the group, was a considerable sum, but fortunately did not take his watch. Then they returned him to the ship, and were quickly lost in the darkness.

"When we reached Panama we went on immediately by rail across the Isthmus and put up at a most curious rambling old hotel, kept by an American woman. She was taller than most men, muscular and square shouldered. She wore a leather belt around her waist, in which were two loaded revolvers, evidently giving her control of the whole place. The hotel was crowded with travelers who had come by a steamship route which ran directly from New Zealand to Panama, and then on to England. These people were waiting to take the steamer which connected with ours from San Francisco, and when we got on board the next day, we found all the passengers from both steamers crowded into the one. Every available space was taken and three or four persons to a room. My husband and I had to part company and I shared a room with my sister and another woman, while Valdemar and my brother with two other men occupied another."

After a month in New York they went to Norway where they were most warmly welcomed and feted everywhere by the hosts of relations. A baby niece born at this time was given the name of Anne Sinclair Faye. One of the sisters gave Anne a pearl ring which had been found in a fish caught in one of the lakes. It evidently had been swallowed by the fish after being lost by some fair lady trailing her hand in the water. I can recall how I loved to think of Aunt Octavia taking the ring off her finger and giving it to her new sister. My dear mother gave me the ring many years later but unfortunately it was stolen from me with other jewels by the maid in a New York hotel.

Their wedding trip included Paris, England and Scotland, where they visited Sinclair relatives. In London they chose furniture and hangings for the Waiawa home. My father had said at the start of the trip, "We won't curtail ourselves, but when we come back we will live on fish and poi."

On their return they were delighted with the two new rooms added to the quaint old house while they were away, consisting of a living room and bedroom. These additions were made in an ingenious manner, facing the garden so as to make a sort of "U" of the house. How happy they were to be at home at quiet Waiawa after seven months of continuous travel, to dream of their adventures in retrospect, and to rejoice in the beginning of a family. Both adored children and eagerly anticipated the advent of the baby coming to them, as did all the natives of Mana, Kekaha, and Poki.

CHAPTER IV

The Saga of Valdemar Knudsen

LEAVING Anne and Valdemar at their peaceful home at Waiawa, let us go back to the Norway of 1779, and try to get some impressions and history of my father's forebears and early life.

My grandfather Presidenten Knudsen was born in the town of Brevig, or Brevik, in 1779. He was related to several of the well-known families such as the Bernhofts and the Adelers, to which family the renowned naval hero Kurt Adeler belonged. After young Knud finished his schooling and education he went to the University of Copenhagen in Denmark. Norway was then a republic and united to Denmark politically, and many young men took advantage of the splendid University training in the city of Copenhagen, as no university had been established in Norway at that time. While he was pursuing his courses at Copenhagen he volunteered in the Danish-Norwegian navy as a lieutenant when the city was attacked by the British in 1807. A vivid painting of this naval battle hangs in the castle of Fredericksborg in Copenhagen.

On his return to Norway soon after this, he was appointed to the office of Presidenten at Christiansand, one of the four cantonments into which Norway was then divided. The title was abolished after his time, and the office became less important. To quote from a letter of my cousin Alexander Seippel, "I send you a miniature of our grandfather which a clever photographer here (Oslo) copied for me from an old daguerrotype probably taken in his early fifties. He was a good clever man, perhaps a little rigid in his opinions, but endowed with sound judgment. I can, for instance, thank him for my name. When I was to be baptised, my sweet and dear mother had been reading a romantic tale, and was inclined to give me the name of Reginald after the hero in the novel. Her father, our grandfather, then came in and said, 'Don't give the boy such a sentimental name! Take rather a gallant name of some hero, call him for instance Alexander.' "

My cousin Alexander Seippel was a favorite nephew of my father, who was very proud of his record. He is now Professor of Sanskrit at the Oslo University, and is said to be the greatest living authority on that language. He is a very outstanding man in European languages as well, and has made great contributions to the knowledge of all ancient languages. In 1936 when I saw him in Oslo at the advanced age of 85 he was busily putting the Scriptures into the vernacular of the Norwegian peasant, a difficult assignment given him by the University of Oslo. While traveling in the Orient some years ago my sister Maud Garstin met a very interesting man who, when talking of ancient languages, heard her speak of her cousin, exclaimed, "Not the *great* Professor Alexander Seippel?", which tribute needless to say was much appreciated by his many relatives.

My grandmother was born on November 27, 1787. Her name was Karen Sophie Svensen, and she came from the inland part of the parish of Holand. She is said to have been quite a beauty, and cousin Alexander wrote in a gallant way, "I think the remarkable beauty of the ladies in the family in Hawaii as well as in Norway may well have been inherited from our grandmother." I can well remember my father speaking with love and admiration of his mother. She was a little lady with lovely features, clear rosy complexion, and quantities of dark wavy hair reaching the floor when she sat on a wee chair. My father was proud of her charming manner which made her beloved by everyone. She had married her first husband Herr Bendiksen at the age of sixteen, and at twenty-one was left a widow with four children. After two years she married Presidenten Knudsen.

It was evidently a comfortable home where these fifteen children were reared. The house was large and had a garden both in front and back, where flowers and shrubs grew in summer, but where only the pine trees showed their green needles in the long cold winters. Many servants, horses and carriages, and sleighs in winter also added to the comfort of their early life. Every year they spent the summer at the country place Björndalen about ten miles out of Christiansand. All my father's happiest memories were centered in this lovely place, which he clothed in romance in his stories to us as children in far off Hawaii.

A century and more has elapsed since Valdemar Knudsen was born in Christiansand (Oslo) on August 5th, 1820. The others of the family were up at Björndalen, the summer home, an hour's drive by carriage. His mother was enjoying the quiet of the big town house, and my grandfather Presidenten Knud Knudsen had come to be with her and see the little new son. As Valdemar was the Presidenten's ninth child, and the eleventh of his mother, there was probably not much excitement about the advent, but it was said that his father was pleased that the baby was a boy. His older brothers were Theodore, Knud, and Julius, and his sisters were Caja, Octavia, Amalia, Camilla, and Ida Constancia, after whom I was named, and who was my father's favorite sister. Of the others I do not remember much except Adelsteen the youngest brother, who made a great pet of me when we all went to Norway in 1882. My father was devoted to his stepbrother Christian Bendikson who was, from all accounts, an unusually fine man and quite the idol of my father in his early life.

In later years, in June 1882, when he and Mama took all of us five youngsters to Norway on a visit to his people, one of the outstanding days was the one on which he drove us out to Björndalen. We wandered through the garden hearing bits of his boyhood adventures. He showed us the pools he fished in for the huge salmon, also the five lovely *roggan*

Knud Knudsen
1771–1852

trees, (known in Scotland as rowan, and in America as the mountain ash) on which we could still trace his initials "V.K." These letters he told us had been carved with his first knife, and had cost him a good thrashing from his father. I can still hear his chuckle as he told us the story, but evidently it made a great impression on him, for I remember distinctly his warnings not to carve our names on tree or stone, not even to write our names on the Pink Terrace in New Zealand where my brother Augustus wanted to put his next to that of the Duke of Edinburgh! He often quoted to us the old saying, "Fools names, like fool's faces, are often seen in public places." I remember too how disgusted my father was to find Uncle Frank and Aunt Isabella Sinclair's name carved on a favorite sandalwood tree near Halemanu in the mountains of Kauai. The place had been lent to them at the time Aunt Isabella was sketching and painting the flowers for her lovely book *The Indigenous Flowers of the Hawaiian Islands*. A feeling of secret pleasure came over me when I heard my father scolding Uncle Frank (who looked very sheepish), and though I loved Uncle Frank I felt he had done wrong and it was right he should be talked to very severely.

Later when I was in Norway, Uncle Adelsteen told me many stories of his adored brother, whose boyhood was full of adventure. He was one of the best on the *ski* amongst his group of friends. He would dash down miles of snow-covered pathways, after having been dragged up by a shaggy little mountain pony, and he was also a famous skater. Once he was fishing through the ice in the bay at Christiansand, and being absorbed by his good luck, did not notice a wind and swell rising. Suddenly a crack hissed in the ice at his feet where he was kneeling beside his fishing hole. Grabbing his dozen or so fish and jumping to his feet, he glided off on his skates, which fortunately he had not unfastened. Scanning the ice between him and the shore, he was able to pick his way between the cracks, and finally reached the shore safely.

One of their great amusements was to get their parents to go sleighing on the ice in the fjord. The horses were shod with special shoes in winter with big spikes to grip into the ice and snow. The boys and girls would hold ropes behind the sleigh and be towed miles on their skates over the thick ice, which often lasted several months in the deep fjords.

Another time he and a friend were hunting *rupa*, or Norwegian grouse up in the mountains near Christiansand. These birds are brown feathered in the summer but grow white plumage in the winter. They are very plentiful about Christmas time, when they are considered a great delicacy, especially when they have been hung a long time! The winter darkness set in before the boys realized it as they were so busy trapping the birds. Suddenly they heard the long drawn-out howl of a wolf! How quickly they grabbed their birds and skied down the long trail, always hearing the howls of the wolves much too near to be comfortable. In those days wolves were a great menace during the long winter months, and my grandfather made Valdemar promise never to be so foolhardy again.

He had another experience with wolves when he was grown up and a student at the University in Oslo. A party of young people planned to go up to Frögneseten one cold frosty afternoon. The big sleighs and sturdy horses decked out with bells on the high standing collars, carried a merry party. After supper and hot "chocolade" they wondered what had become of the old fiddler who was to play for the dancing. Fearing he had lost his way in the snow, three of the young men, led by Valdemar, volunteered to search for him, and set out towards the neighboring village. As the young rescuers tramped through the woods they heard in the distance the sound of a violin. Suddenly it stopped and immediately the horrid sound of a wolf's howl came to their ears. Realizing that the wind was blowing towards them, and that they were safe from giving the scent of their advance to the wolf, they went silently on as fast as possible. The music grew louder as they came to the edge of a small clearing in the center of which stood a wood-cutter's shack. What a scene it was that met my father's eyes, as the bright moonlight showed so clearly the old musician perched on the roof of the shack, and fiddling literally for dear life, with three wolves sitting around waiting for him to become exhausted, and collapse with cold and fatigue. The poor man had taken refuge on the roof of the hut when the wolves chased him, and had discovered that they were fascinated by the sound of his violin. Carefully, the young men took aim with their pistols, killing two, and scaring the other off, whereupon they rescued the poor old fiddler who was quite worn out, as he had been playing there in the cold and in great fear for several hours. Giving him a drink of cognac, the young fellows half carried him back to Frögneseten where the young folks made much of him as the hero of the evening. Soon he was quite recovered and insisted on playing for the dancing. When the time came to return to Oslo, they drove him back to the city, where he became the toast of the town. When I asked my father about it later he said he had never told us the story fearing it would frighten us. He acknowledged the part he took in the adventure, but disclaimed being the hero Uncle Adelsteen made him out to be.

Valdemar made his mark at the University. He shared a room with his brother Theodore, two years his senior and his greatest pal. They were both great linguists, and always conversed in Latin, preferring it to their mother tongue. Beside Latin my father spoke German, French, Italian, and Spanish fluently, and his English was perfect even though he always retained a slight foreign accent. He was a great admirer of the English language, and once told me he would rather have been a subject of Great Britain than of any other nation, because the constitution and laws of England were so admirable.

One spring morning while he and Theodore were chatting with some charming ladies who had drawn up to the sidewalk in their carriage, Valdemar thoughtlessly put his foot on one of the spokes of the wheel. The spirited horse took fright and before the coachman could control the animal, Valdemar's leg, which had slipped between the spokes, was badly twisted at the knee, and he was thrown to the ground. After weeks of suffering he was allowed to sit with the leg straight out before him on a long stool by the window. While he went on with his studies, he spent most of his summer in an invalid's chair. For amusement he used to practice shooting at a target on a nearby tree with his cherished wee pistol. He became splendidly proficient, thinking nothing of putting his bullets one right on top of another in the bull's eye. In fact he had such good aim his friends called him the Devil's Marksman. This gift stood him in good stead many a time in his later life.

The following winter he and Theodore went in their own sleigh to their older step-brother, Christian Bendiksen's wedding. My father's memories of his step-brother, many years his senior, were of a splendid and handsome man. In fact he spoke of him in such an enthusiastic way that I always thought of Uncle Christian as a sort of fairy prince, and of the story of going to his wedding as particularly fascinating and romantic. My mother, too, corroborated this impression for she had been immediately won by Christian's charm and goodness and by his lovely family life when she had met him on her wedding trip.

As Valdemar and Theodore started out to this wonderful event, the first brother's wedding in the family, the weather was perfect, clear and cold, and the snow hard and marvelous for sleighing. They skimmed along, reaching the big country house in less than three hours. There they immediately got into a round of gaieties; a Norwegian wedding often had festivities lasting over a week. Valdemar's knee had healed crookedly, his leg standing out at quite an angle so that dancing was out of the question, but he joined as best he could in the fun and frolic. However, it was very disappointing to him as he had always been so active and such a leader in all sports and games. Consequently after the wedding he and Theodore decided they had had enough of festival and, slipping off, they got their sleigh and horses and started for Oslo. A storm seemed brewing, and before they had gone half way, snow began falling heavily, blocking part of the road which led through an open valley. The horses were forced to a standstill, and the best the boys could do was to tramp down the snow in front of the horses and move them along a few yards at a time. This was slow work, but they took turns, and just as they were getting out of the soft drifts there was a loud crack and Valdemar's crooked knee went straight! He was so astonished at the sudden and complete recovery of his leg that he began jumping up and down in the snow in the greatest excitement. There was not the slightest pain, and never did he have, even in after years, any trouble with that leg or knee. Often as he told us of the adventure he always ended by saying: "That trip to my brother's wedding was the best thing that ever happened to me in Norway."

After finishing his University course, he began the study of medicine, but after a year's trial he was advised by the medical faculty to give it up, as he could not stand the sight of blood, and was continually brought out of the dissecting room in a dead faint, to have water pumped on his head in the square on which the hospital and medical college stood.

To please his father he then began the study of law, but evidently did not go far with that, for he shortly after decided to go to America. This was a great sorrow to his parents and to Theodore. However, the latter joined him in New York a couple of years later. I do not remember just what my father did at first, but it was something in the custom house. He soon joined a publishing house with a man named Garrigue. This Mr. Garrigue and his wife were charming people who often invited him to their home. They remained staunch friends all his life. I remember meeting them in 1882, also Mrs. Garrigue's sister Harriet who married Uncle Theodore and so became our Aunt Harriet. Their children and the Garrigues were interesting young people. One of the Garrigue girls married Professor Masaryk and lived in Prague, where we visited them in the summer of 1884.

After the World War of 1914–1918, Professor Masaryk was elected President of Czechoslovakia and was a wonderful leader of that country. This later bit of history reminded me of my father's admiration for the handsome brown-eyed young professor who was so cordial and interesting to us in 1884, and I remember my father saying, "We will hear from that young man before many years pass."

To return to Valdemar's early life in New York and his connection with the publishing house, which afterwards became the firm of Henry Holt and Co., Valdemar's gift for languages made him a great asset to the firm. He was soon making business trips through the eastern states, and becoming acquainted with numbers of people. At one time he was several months in Poughkeepsie, where he stayed with friends of Mr. Garrigue's. Every one who knew him spoke of his personality, and in later years I found the old friends of Kauai and Honolulu devoted to him.

His life in New York was a most busy one, and having Theodore with him was a great joy. At this time he bought from a vendor on Broadway a tiny squirrel or a chipmunk which was a pet he came to adore. He could always give us a new story of his little "Squigee", which he taught many tricks. It would scamper to him the moment he opened the door, and soon learned, and never made a mistake, that he kept nuts in his right coat pocket. This was the cause of its death, as one day Valdemar came home early with a cold, and lying down on his bed to read, did not play with his little pet as usual. He dropped off to sleep, and during his nap must have turned over on his right side. On awaking and calling for "Squigee" there was no sign of the little animal, and then he was horrified to find it still warm but suffocated in his coat pocket. As children we all used to feel terribly sad over this story, for Papa certainly convinced us of his love for the bright and interesting wee pet, and of how desolate he was over its loss.

After Theodore's marriage, Valdemar returned to Norway on a visit to his father and mother. He tried hard to decide to remain in his Fatherland, especially for his parents' sake. However he found everything so narrow and limited, with no scope for new business ventures, that he returned to New York where he went on with his business association with Mr. Garrigue, who offered him a partnership. But the lure of California in that historic year of 1849 decided him to go adventuring to the far west, not by the covered wagon trail, but around Cape Horn. It always seemed to me that he never got the wonder and the fascination of California out of his mind. He knew Colonel Sutter (later, general), and many other of the outstanding men of those days. In *Sutter's Gold* by Blaise Cendrars, my father's impressions are confirmed. He too felt with Colonel Sutter, that California's best future lay in agriculture and developing the land, and, like the renowned colonel, was not drawn to the actual mining, though he tried his hand at it for a time. Colonel Sutter had built his lovely home "The Hermitage" on the Feather River north of Sacramento and doubtless he and Valdemar fraternized, as the Swiss and Norwegians have much in common, and they lived comparatively near each other. I am sure my father would have been enthralled over *Sutter's Gold* as it is a most fascinating tale and should be read by everyone in order to understand those early days.

One of the stories my father told of his first experiences in camping out in the wild canyons and mountains was of much amusement to us and to him in retrospect. Rolled up in their blankets he and his "pard" were asleep under a liveoak tree, when they were awakened by the most unearthly yells coming from the place where they had cooked their supper. Convinced they heard Indians, they lay absolutely quiet, afraid to move lest they be discovered, and waited till the noise abated. What was their chagrin to discover the next morning the footprints of coyotes which had been fighting over the remains of the supper! Although a lover of animals, Valdemar declared the coyote was a hateful creature, a feeling shared by all Californians.

After some mining experiences and exploring the country he decided to start a trading and supply agency at the fork of the Feather and Yuba Rivers, with headquarters at Sacramento. It was a beautiful place with liveoaks growing all around, and the rivers dashing by. He loved the place and life, and made a great success of the venture. Business called him often to Sacramento and farther afield to San Francisco. He had a strongly built house with a safe, to which the miners came continually to deposit their gold dust until it could be taken to the city. In this way, he established a sort of clearing house or branch bank of an informal nature. One of my father's most thrilling stories of this time was of two very agreeable men who came one afternoon asking for a night's shelter. Valdemar was delighted, as was everyone in those days, to have company. After the men had refreshed themselves, they sat out under the liveoaks, and the conversation turned to pistols, guns, and marksmanship. Valdemar told them of his accident during his college days, and of how, to pass the tedious hours of convalescence, he had become an expert shot. The men asked him to shoot again and again at any small object —a tiny yellow leaf, a bit of white bark at a distance. When they retired, my father, carrying his trusty pistol at his belt, called his black and tan spaniel, saying "Beauty is never happy unless she sleeps at my feet." Next morning the two men went on their way, and my father was left alone again as his partner had gone to San Francisco on business. On his return a few days later, the partner told of the great excitement over the capture of two notorious robbers. He had seen them being taken to the gallows, and was astonished to have one of them call out to him: "Aren't you the partner of that Norwegian up at the Feather and Yuba Rivers?" Upon the partner acknowledging the recognition, the robber went on to say: "Well, give him my regards, and tell him we were prepared to open his safe, and if it had not been for his magnificent shooting and his damned little dog he would have been robbed the night we were there." This news astounded Valdemar as they were such cultivated men that he had thoroughly enjoyed their company without in the least suspecting their motives in begging a night's shelter.

My father did not confine his interests to his own business, for he took an active part in the civic affairs of California. He was a delegate to the Constitutional Convention which made California a state of the Union, and in 1850 and 1851 was one of the Vigilantes who took it upon themselves to drive out of California the vicious criminals and murderers who were making the new state a dangerous spot for honest people.

On his return to Norway in 1852 he was fortunately in time to see his mother again. She died shortly after his arrival. Though he felt he should remain with his father in his declining years, the call of California was too strong, and one day he began packing up his belongings. His father came into the room, and seeing what he was doing, asked if he were returning to America. My father acknowledged his plan, and told the old presidenten of his longing for the new country. "I knew you could not be happy here, my son," said the old man. "Go and take up your life there, but keep a thought for your old father who probably will not see you again in this world." Valdemar always blessed his father for making the parting so easy. Shortly after his return to California he heard of his father's death, and his last message, "Write to Valdemar I send him my loving greeting."

After Valdemar's arrival in New York he took passage for Panama and then went overland across the Isthmus to take the boat on the Pacific side. On the way he contracted Panama fever, and was left for dead by his companions in a little village. Here he was tended by an old native woman. What she did for him he never knew, but on his recovery from the delirium she whispered to him not to worry, she had taken his money belt and hidden it safely for him. He remained with the old woman for several months, and she took the best of care of him, always keeping most of the goat's milk for him, which he declared saved his life, as it was so easily digested, and strengthening. Of course he rewarded her handsomely, and went on to Acapulco with a band of rollicking young Irishmen. A schooner was lying in the bay, and Valdemar finally persuaded the captain to give them passage, so off the dare-devil company of young men sailed, and Valdemar got safely back to his beloved place at the Feather and Yuba Rivers.

For a year the after-effects of the Panama fever kept him feeling rather miserable, and finally he took a doctor's advice to go to a warm climate and rid himself of the symptoms. He took passage in a boat going south to Mexico, and was moving his baggage on board when he heard the captain's wife, a regular virago, cursing and swearing and using the vilest language. Feeling he could not stand the strain of such a creature on board, he got back his money and wandered down the waterfront till he saw a ship with the sign "Sailing for Hilo." On enquiring of the captain and hearing they were to leave the next day, Valdemar decided then and there to take the trip and, leaving his partner and his agent in charge, he sailed away for the tropic isles. He expected to return to California in a year's time, but the Fates had other plans for him, and for his whole future life in the Sandwich Islands.

Evidently navigation was not the captain's strong point, for on coming ashore Valdemar found himself at the little harbor of Koloa, Kauai, instead of in Hilo, Hawaii. In his search for health it really made no difference to him, and though he did not recognize it at the time, the hand of Fate was guiding him to his future home. Leaving his few pieces of baggage on the so-called wharf, he started to walk up the road, enjoying the cool trade wind and the new sights. Under the shade of a kukui tree he found an old Hawaiian man resting, by his side his shoulder pole and two large calabashes which were slung in the native hand-made mesh of *olona*, the strongest fibre known to the primitive Hawaiians. Valdemar sat down with the greeting "Aloha" which he had learned, and before long was writing in his note book all the words the Hawaiian told him. Touching the calabash he learned it was *umeke;* a stone, *Pohaku;* himself, *haole;* etc. With his quick ear and gift for languages he immediately got the correct pronunciation, and won the native's aloha and admiration. When Mr. Gilmore of Koloa village came driving down he found the newcomer holding quite a conversation, though I suppose with more gestures then words. Mr. Gilmore introduced himself and kindly invited the *malihini* to drive to the harbor for his bags and return to the Gilmore home for a stay. Valdemar accepted at once, and was always grateful for such hospitality.

Shortly after Valdemar's arrival at Koloa he met Mr. and Mrs. Marshall. The Marshalls, the manager of Lihue Plantation, were living at Malumalu, near Lihue, and became Valdemar's life-long friends. Later, the charming coterie of congenial friends in this locality was eulogized by Sanford Dole as follows: "Among the memories of Kauai one of the most unforgettable is of that remarkable little group of kindred spirits that dwelt at or near Malumalu. One of these was James Marshall who later won the honor and title of general in the Civil War. Another at Malumalu was Admiral Reynolds, also Judge Bond, and Judge Hardy. These men and their wives were people of high ideals and large attainments who lived near each other in congenial intimacy and freedom from care." In this group Valdemar Knudsen was included, and visited with the Marshalls often. He was made assistant to Mr. Marshall, but in a year's time he turned to west Kauai for a home, the dry climate at Kekaha and Poki suiting his health much better.

At Kekaha he met and liked a Mr. Archibald Archer of Scotch-Norwegian parentage. From him, and from his partner Mr. Gruben, Valdemar bought the lease of Poki, and later the leases of Kekaha and Mana. He started a horse and cattle ranch, also an orchard at Waiawa, where he built a comfortable home. His exhibitions of corn, fruit, and other crops grown at Waiawa are noted in the annals of the Royal Agricultural Society in Honolulu. He collected many varieties of bananas from all over the Pacific, grew and roasted coffee, and planted a fine grove of mangoes. His growing of grapes and making of wine also attracted much attention, and he was very successful in this venture. Years later, in 1888, when visiting with General and Mrs. Marshall near Boston, we young members of the Knudsen family had the opportunity of sampling a bottle of this wine. A parting gift from my father when they left the islands, one cobweb-covered bottle had been reserved by the dear old General who brought it up from his cellar for this special celebration.

Soon after settling at Waiawa my father heard, through a legal friend in San Francisco that his partner had absconded. This man who owed so much to Valdemar had sold all the property at the Feather and Yuba Rivers and had disappeared, an easy thing to do in those early California days. The mails were so irregular, sometimes six months between vessels, that Valdemar decided there was no redress to be had, and accepted his loss with good grace.

Fortunately, Valdemar was happy and contented in his new environment. His friends were true, and delightfully cordial, and the attributes of his personality, interest in science and languages always won him a distinct place in the social, business, and political life of the Islands. He was deeply religious, and always went to Father Damon's "Bethel" when in Honolulu. He sympathized with all religious effort, and was always ready to give what he could. His outstanding work along such lines was his care and training of young boys at his home at Waiawa, a sort of continuation school for these young men, whom he inculcated with the highest ideals. The names I recall him mentioning are Kahu Kanoa, son of the Governor of Kauai, David Kua, who became one of my father's right hand men,

Charlie Storrbach, of German extraction, and Henry Archer, a son of Archibald Archer.

Young Kanoa studied law and government, and then had some years further training in Honolulu with Judge Lee, who was a warm friend of my father's. Later he was much rejoiced when Kahu Kanoa was appointed judge of the Waimea district, and came to live in the house which is now the parsonage at Waimea. I remember going there sometimes after the long services in the old Waimea stone church where huge conclaves of natives congregated, sitting on the floor while my parents and the older children sat on a bench. I think we often, perhaps semi-monthly, came into Waimea for the services. I remember Kahu's wife very well, and that we liked being at her house to rest after church. In 1874 Judge Kanoa, at my father's request, was able to accommodate the members of the expedition which came to observe the Transit of Venus.

Charlie Storrbach became a trusted cowboy, of whom more later, and Henry Archer, showing a marked ability for mechanics, was sent to Boston probably to Mr. Peirce, for an engineering course. He did remarkably well, but like all tropic-born people was unaware of the need of care and extra warm clothing in that climate. He contracted a cold which developed into pneumonia, and he died far from his native shore, much to Valdemar's sorrow. David Kua married a sweet girl from his own village of Poki, and raised a fine family of boys and girls and was always of great assistance on the ranch.

Valdemar was a fearless rider, and enjoyed the ranch life to the fullest. His many horses were well trained. He thought nothing of the long horseback rides to see his friends, the McBrides near Eleele, the Smiths at Koloa, or on to Lihue to the Rices, Marshalls, Reynolds, etc. His activities in securing botanical specimens brought him in close touch with Dr. Hillebrand, who lived in Honolulu where the Foster Gardens on Nuuanu Avenue now are. Dr. Hillebrand often visited at Waiawa to inspect the specimens Valdemar had found, and to go collecting with the latter in the mountains. It was Dr. Hillebrand who brought many of our lovely flowering trees, and other shrubs and trees to the islands, and interested many of the leading botanists of Europe to come to the islands in search of new ferns, flowers and trees. Valdemar Knudsen's name was well known to them all, as over a dozen species were named *Knudseni*, due to his discovery of them. He later became acquainted with Remy, Wawra and Brigham. The last two did not become the fast friends the others had with my father, for two distinct reasons. Wawra was taken by my father when I was a small child to see a very beautiful tree which was unnamed and which my father knew was unknown to botanists. Wawra took the specimens which my father and mother had pressed so carefully, and afterwards wrote back he had named the tree *Wawraensi*. I can hear to this day my mother's denouncement of the tricky old Austrian botanist! Professor Brigham visited Waiawa about 1864, and Valdemar assisted him in every way, even taking him to Niihau, where he was introduced to the Sinclairs, with whom Valdemar had by this time established an intimate friendship. Another trip was arranged for him a year later, and when my father heard it was taken for the express purpose of a proposal of marriage to Miss Anne Sinclair, he said, "If I had had any idea of Brigham's designs, I certainly would not have run the risk of having him as my rival."

The Hawaiians on his holdings were devoted to *Kanuka* (Knudsen) and later often called him *makua* (father). The old law of the land ordered that each man work three days a week for the *haku* (master) or *konohiki* (overseer). This was their rental money. On other days, they planted taro or sweet potatoes and yams, fished, or did anything they chose for themselves. Having between three and four hundred Hawaiians of all ages to call on, he always had enough labor for his needs on the ranch for fence building, driving and branding cattle, breaking horses, and butchering once a month. The old men were kept back to care for the garden and the home taro patches and to keep the several springs clear. One of these springs with sweet bubbling water was called the King's Well.

After visiting with his tenants at Poki and Kekaha, my father would invariably, from the very first year he lived at Waiawa, ride down to Pupupakai to bathe and swim in the one quiet reef-protected lagoon on the whole coast from Waimea to Polihale. The salt water always invigorated him, and with the constant outdoor life and sunshine he soon lost all symptoms of his fever, and recovered his vim and enthusiasm for everything.

Long before the arrival of the Sinclairs, he had been chosen by the king as one of his nobles, and was always present in the capitol for every session of the legislature. The title of noble corresponded to that of senator today, the difference being that the nobles were appointed by the king. During these visits in Honolulu he saw much of the Thomas Browns, who had left Waialua Falls Mansion and their coffee venture, and after several years in the Eastern states had settled in Honolulu. It was told that young Mr. von Holt, who was paying court to Miss Alice Brown, was very jealous of him before winning the hand of the lovely Miss Alice. Valdemar knew every one, and was devoted to Kamehameha IV, and Queen Emma, as everyone was. Princess Bernice Pauahi Bishop and Mr. Charles R. Bishop were also great friends.

At Waiawa he had his books and a monthly magazine which he passed on to other members of the Exchange Magazine Club, and he had his boys to look after and train. One day Charlie Storrback came limping in with a hole in the sole of his foot the size of the end of a pencil. No sign of the stick which had caused the damage was to be seen, and the blood had stopped, leaving the wound quite clean. Valdemar was suspicious of something being still left in the wound, so he made the boy sit down with his foot in a bucket of hot salted water which was reheated and replaced often. After several hours the foot seemed to shrink and became very wrinkled, when suddenly out popped a bit of the stick quite half an inch long. The foot was then well bandaged and by the next day was practically healed. This was an old Norwegian method of dealing with such wounds, and Valdemar had seen it used among the farm hands on his father's country estate. Old Kaluahi, the medicine *kahuna*, who lived on the hill back of Waiawa and just above the King's Well, approved of this treatment, and said that he had used it frequently, and Papa was glad of his help and backing.

One evening a fine old native from the village came up about seven o'clock with his pretty daughter, who was an *ehu*, a fair Hawaiian with a rather rosy complexion and a glint of reddish gold in her hair. After some preliminary conversation, her father asked if he would like to have his daughter for wife, as he would gladly give her to him. The Hawaiians he said, did not like to see him living alone without a woman, so he had brought the girl along and would leave her at Waiawa if Kanuka would agree. Difficult and embarrassing as it was with the pretty blushing girl present, her eyes cast down, and yet seemingly quite approving her father's idea, Kanuka finally got them to understand that he could not agree to the plan, and they went away very non-plussed.

Many were the chances he had of collecting old Hawaiian spears, calabashes, idols, dog-tooth dancing ornaments, etc. One prized gift from Governor Kanoa, a beautiful black kauwila wood spear with a carved loose ball within four bands of carved wood, he stuck over his door from veranda eave to the wall, where it remained several years. Every native that came up to speak to Kanuka would crawl in awe under this spear on hands and knees, so it evidently had a great reputation as the King's spear. Unfortunately yeilding to the importunate request of a gentleman who had brought letters from Mr. Henry A. Peirce of Boston, he gave it away, thinking he could get another, but he could never find one.

Anne Sinclair
c. 1875

Valdemar Knudsen
c. 1875
Bishop Museum Photo

He had many good friends among the Hawaiians. I have already mentioned Kaluahi who lived on the hill, and was a real medicine *kahuna*. He helped Papa in many ways, especially in controlling the younger men. Then there was Kanaikino, the teacher out at Mana, who had forty children in his school. He came to Waiawa for the books for his children, supplies etc., as Valdemar was agent for the Board of Education for Kekaha, Poki, and Mana for many years.

In those early days, land was very cheap. There was no way of watering or irrigating the fields, and the grass became absolutely parched and dead during the dry months. Cattle often died for want of food and water. There was no market for beef and no ice to ship it on if there had been a market. The hides and tallow were the only articles which could be exported on sailing vessels. The present-day criticisms that men in those days stole or bought lands from the unsuspecting natives for a song are not true. The land belonged to the Crown, the Crown Commissioners advised the King, and the sum asked was what was determined as the current value of the land. This plan was made by the missionaries, Mr. Armstrong, Dr. Lowell Smith, Mr. Alexander, Mr. Richards, and that great statesman and leader, Dr. Gerrit Judd. Perhaps in the very early days there had been instances of fraud, but when my father came here in 1853 and the Sinclairs in 1863, all was well organized, and leases and sales of Government and Crown lands were drawn up and executed in the most legal and approved way. The leasehold of the Crown lands of Kekaha, Poki, and Mana were held at $1500.00 a year, and it was often difficult for Valdemar to make enough to pay this rental and have any funds left over. With the tremendous impetus of the Reciprocity Treaty in 1876, largely brought about by Mr. Paul Isenberg, money came in from outside investors, water was brought in flumes and ditches, and pumped from wells and artesian wells, which made the dusty acres blossom with sugar cane, rice, etc. Tremendous courage and foresight, and immense financial outlays were necessary, and no one in the present day can even guess at the hardships and struggles. Paul Isenberg had, on his arrival, come to Valdemar for a job, and they became fast friends. He was a very clever and far-seeing man, who did much for the islands. (See *Koamalu* by Ethel Damon.)

Of course the lands of Poki, Kekaha, Mana, and Niihau are now valuable properties, but in the early days of the fifties and sixties it took great courage and vision to see the possibility of such growth and expansion as the fostering of great markets for sugar, beef, and wool, or of the fleets of vessels that later sprang into the service of the ranchers and planters.

In 1864 with the arrival of the Sinclairs on Niihau, Valdemar was enthusiastic in helping them settle there. He had become a true *kamaaina* and his ten years' experience was of great assistance to Frank and James Sinclair. In 1865 life began to have a new meaning for him, and in 1866 he found romance on Niihau when he won the hand of Anne Sinclair. Strange indeed that he, coming from far Norway, and she from Scotland and New Zealand, should find each other in these isles of the Pacific and here begin their united life.

CHAPTER V

Waiawa

WHEN on April 11th, 1868, a daughter was born at 1:00 A.M., the news spread swiftly, and many were the Hawaiian visitors who came to see the fair haired baby. Much to Anne's astonishment, and Valdemar's amusement, they were then told by one of their older *konohiki* men, that all the natives were much relieved to know of the birth of a child to Anne. They had been most apprehensive that Kanuka had something vitally wrong with him as he had never wanted a wahine, or mistress, as most of the white men did, and they had really felt distressed on Anne's account, thinking of her future disappointment in perhaps never having a family. Aunt Helen Robinson was the nurse and Dr. James W. Smith of Koloa came in time for the arrival of the baby. A thirty-five or forty mile horseback ride over the sometimes impassable roads, streams and rivers, was not an easy undertaking, and when the doctor came at the date expected, he was prepared to wait. In one instance it was three weeks, a great mortification to the prospective mother. Before Dr. Smith, who was also a *kahuna pule*, (clergyman) left the house he was called upon to baptise the new baby who received the name of Ida Elizabeth Knudsen. The first name was after her Norwegian aunt in Dramen, Norway, Mrs. Ida Constancia Faye, and Elizabeth after her maternal grandmother, Mrs. Francis Sinclair of Makaweli and Niihau. The wee girl was to have been baptised Ida Constancia but Aunt Helen let it be known that Grandmama Sinclair would be terribly hurt if her name was not given to the child. It does not sound like Grandmama, but shows how families in those days made such a fuss over the naming of a child!

When his small daughter was three weeks old, Valdemar was called to Honolulu for the opening of the Legislature, of which he was an active member. To break the long journey over to take passage on the schooner at Lihue, he put up at Judge and Mrs. McBride's hospitable home. That evening the terrible earthquake of 1868 took place! As soon as it was over, Valdemar roped and saddled his horse and rode back to Waiawa. Anne was greatly touched, and happy to see him. Assuring himself that all was well he started again early next day, caught the packet to Honolulu and attended the session which lasted five or six weeks. On his return he took Anne and the baby over to Niihau. Little Ida, though only two and a half months old, stood the trip splendidly and was shown off proudly to her grandmother. In late August of the same year when not quite five months old she was carried on horseback up the long four-hour trip to Halemanu, where Anne and Valdemar reveled in the cool mountain air.

The following May 26, 1869, a new baby came, Augustus Francis, and on October 18, 1870, another daughter, Maud, was welcomed, Ida then being but two and a half years old. It was told of her that on hearing her baby sister's first cry, she looked up at her nurse, Haleaka, and remarked, *Kao* (goat). At the back of Waiawa House there were always numbers of wild goats running on the rocks and cliffs and a little kid's bleating sounds very much like the cry of a tiny baby.

A tremendous Kona storm had raged, absolutely preventing Dr. Smith from coming to attend my mother. My sister Maud tells me she once heard from Aunt Helen that my father called in the Hawaiian medical *kahuna*, Kaluahi, who delivered the baby with coconut oil on his carefully washed fingers. I never heard the story myself but it is very plausible, and most interesting. Fortunately my mother's health was abounding and she adored her growing family, being constantly helped by her husband, who was adept in the duties of the normal care of children.

The big storm was over and the grass was dry enough for Augustus and myself to be allowed to play on the lawn while Haleaka sat in the shade of the house watching us. Suddenly the wee boy ran across a bank of mud which had been deposited there during the storm. It had caked over, but he sank into the soft mud below. I can still see him, his little skirt and panties filthy black as Haleaka drew him out. Mama, standing at the living room window, saw it all and was much amused at my canny waiting on the clean grass. I was very proud of myself for taking such good care of my shoes and socks. Papa never allowed us to go barefoot except on the beaches; the parched earth and rocks near the house would almost burn our feet in the summer.

With no water led into the house or the garden, all grass and flowers withered in the long summer months when no rain fell. Fortunately the "King's Well," fed from underground sources, never went dry nor even diminished in volume. There we procured all water for drinking and household purposes, and one man was detailed to bring over two calabashes full slung on a shoulder pole, many times a day. Papa and Mama often took us over to see the well, and we always had a drink in an inverted taro leaf cup, which we were taught to make early in our lives. From such cups the water, a silvery sparkle, tasted doubly good. For bathing we had later a big redwood tub in a little thatched bathhouse in the garden, where Papa dug a well and installed a hand pump. As we grew older we had to take turns at pumping and I remember how tired my arms were after we had got the tub two-thirds full. Mama would drive us to the beach a mile away several times a week, and how we loved crowding in the little basket phaeton with the horse, Hikili, to draw us, and to run on the cool sands and wade in the lovely ocean waves as they came up on the beach. Sometimes Papa could get off, so we would take our supper, and just get home in time to be popped into bed.

One evening when Mama was alone in the house, Papa being in Honolulu at the Legisture and the servants all gone home to their village, she heard a light foot-fall coming down the long lanai—step-step-step—too light for an adult or even a child, though very definite. She looked up from her sewing to watch the doorway where the lamplight streamed out, but just then the sound ceased and no one appeared, though she carried the lamp out and looked up and down. The next morning she asked the servants about it, thinking a child might have strayed from home, but they were terrified and assured her it must have been an *akua* (spirit). A few nights later the same thing happened, but this time Mama carried her lamp through to the solid door in the dining room, and waited there with her hand on the knob. As the step-step-step came steadily nearer even her stout heart must have quailed a little, but nevertheless she opened the door as the sound came opposite, thrust out the light, and—up flew a great *auku* (sea bird) out and away across the garden.

In the early seventies Grandmama Sinclair bought the lands of Makaweli and Hanapepe, Kauai, and a little later built what is still known as Makaweli House. The altitude, eighteen hundred feet, the lovely forest, hills and valleys, the flowers, especially roses, all over the veranda and porch, reminded Anne poignantly of the old Craigforth House in New Zealand. Grandmama, who disliked the heat on Niihau during the summer, always felt Makaweli was her true home.

Many of my most vivid memories are connected with Niihau and a crossing in 1874 remains clear in every detail. The large whale boat bought by Uncle Frank Sinclair when the family first settled on Niihau, still plied regularly between that island and Kauai on weekly trips for mail, *paiai* (poi before softening and straining) and provisions, and many were the voyages taken to visit Grandmama. The boatmen were all Hawaiians captained by a splendid specimen by the name of Taiwi, and these trips were quite an

Makaweli House
Home of the Sinclairs and Robinsons
Bishop Museum Photo

old story to me at six years of age! The crossings usually took from four to five hours and I can still hear my father's voice saying, "Have patience, we will soon be there" and feel his sympathetic pat when I had been violently ill over the side of the boat. A story told of me when I was so small I could only lisp, was that when I was begging and clamoring for something, my cousin Eliza Gay admonished me to "have patience." To this reproof I replied with great spirit, "I'se dot patience," and when the grownups laughingly asked me where I had learned patience, I replied, "In the Niihau boat." They one and all agreed it was a mighty good place to practice that virtue.

On this special trip in 1874 there were four children: myself, six years old; Augustus, five years; Maud, three and a half years; and Eric, about eighteen months old. I must try and make you all see the picture of our journey. First we were awakened at 2 A.M., dressed and bundled onto a mattress laid in the bottom of a little express wagon. I was too excited with the eerie adventure to sleep and I recall the brilliant moonlight and dark shadows, my parents sitting on the front seat with little Eric asleep in my mother's arms, and the arrival at Pupupakai three miles away, below where the Kekaha Sugar Mill now stands. Taiwi was waiting for us, tall, stalwart, a perfect specimen of Hawaiian manhood with nothing on but a *malo* (loincloth). He greeted us with a smile on his handsome, kindly face. His men were asleep on the sand and after he had talked long and earnestly with Papa and Mama we were finally told to go to sleep on the floor of the little bathhouse where the mattress had been placed. At daylight we were wakened, given some bread and butter and carried pick-a-back by the natives to the boat which had been launched. We children were so accustomed to that sort of travel we took it all as a matter of course.

In later years Mama told me that when she had remonstrated with Taiwi for not starting at the original hour planned, he had said with his winning smile, "*Auwe* Annie,

Knudsen Family Group
Vienna 1885
Seated l to r: Eric, Arthur, Valdemar
Standing l to r: Ida, Maud, Augustus

the *nalu* (surf) is too high. It would be all right for you and Kanuka but if the boat capsized with the *keikis* on board we might not find them in the dark water and high surf." He then most graphically showed her with his hands how they would go feeling about under the waves for her babies. She declared that was enough to convince her he was right, and she then did not care how long we waited for the *nalu* to go down.

The landing through the surf at Kii after our five hour trip is an intensely vivid memory. I can still see Taiwi up in the stern of the boat, steering with his oar and calling "*ho-i, ho-i*" (pull, pull) to the men when he saw the right moment to strain on the oars; his quick glance backwards to watch the oncoming breakers and his skill in evading the moment when the wave would break over the boat, then the rush in to the quiet water inside the reef, the boat pulled near to shore by ropes thrown to the crowd on the beach, and our being carried up and left above the reach of the tide.

Cousin George Gay was there to meet us with a carriage, a pair of horses, and innumerable cowboys to assist. Soon we had our faces washed and were ready for our long delayed breakfast. The coffee was on the campfire and sweet potatoes baking in the ashes and a demijohn of milk cooling in the well for us. Suddenly Cousin George, who was a marvelous fisherman, ran to the reef with rod and line and in one throw brought up a shining, silvery *moi* which he deftly cleaned right there in a salty pool. Then splitting it on a stick he broiled the fish and in less time than it takes to tell the story we were all feasting on that delicious *moi*. It was the best thing I ever tasted and I seem to still enjoy its flavor in memory after sixty years!

Breakfast over we all started off for "The House," a two hour drive over the lovely rolling grassy plains where countless sheep roamed. We passed an ewe and Mama called to us to look at her wee newborn lamb, whereupon Eric very seriously remarked, "It's awfully born," which sage remark

Kii Landing, Niihau
Principal Winter Landing
Bishop Museum Photo

from the eighteen months old little boy became a byword in the family for any animal weak and wobbly. As we drew near the gate and up the avenue of the yellow flowered monkey pod trees all in blossom and scenting the air, we soon arrived at "The House," finding our precious grandmother waiting with open arms for her dear ones and the new grandson Eric whom she had not yet seen. There she stood, a little slim woman of 74, beautiful and fascinating in her dainty dress and with her lace cap showing under her shirred silk bonnet. We ran to her, she was our dearest one of all the family, and though we greeted and loved the others—Aunt Jean, Aunt Helen, Uncle Frank and Aunt Isabella—it was to Grandmama we turned at all times. She spoiled us, I suppose, but we were a pretty manageable lot of youngsters and in those days children truly were "seen but not heard!" Once little Maud said something and her teasing cousin Eliza immediately took her up, saying, "Well, and why are you making a remark?" Maud meekly replied, "Oh I didn't mean it for a remark," which answer turned the tables on Eliza much to my satisfaction and, as I quickly sensed, to Grandmama's as well!

"The House" was situated on a bluff with a fine view of the shore as far as to the landing at Nonopapa and in the distance the tiny island of Kaula, ten miles to the southwest. Life on Niihau was full of interest to us all. The older ones walked to the shore about a half mile distant every other day to find the beautiful shells washed up on the beaches, and we vied with each other in making really fine collections. During my childhood we found many rare specimens both on Niihau and on Kauai at Waiele Beach below and west of Waiawa. I can remember riding through a big swamp, almost an inland sea, to reach the beach land and we often had to lift our feet in the stirrups up almost along the horses' necks while our horses plodded and waded after Papa's horse. He told us then of the Hawaiians going by canoe from Mana to Waimea when he first came to live at Waiawa, and that they would tie their canoes to the coconut trees on the bank of this tremendous swamp when they wanted to see him or Kaluahi. The *neke*, a reed, grew luxuriantly along the edges where wading birds made their nests by the thousands.

The stilt-bird, *aieo*, named *Knudsenii* after him and the mudhen, *alae*, were the most numerous though we often saw the *kolea*, and the Hawaiian duck. The natives often brought us the mud hen's eggs, a great delicacy. As we rode and drove along the hard sand land towards Waiele to picnic and look for shells we were constantly amused by the stilt-birds flying and wheeling and screeching above us or feigning a broken wing or leg to lure us away from their nests.

Papa finally got the half-finished Waiele ditch dug through and led the bulk of the water off. There were distinct signs of ancient trials to get a ditch dug and a legend was told that the Menehunes had worked on this project but in their zeal had worked too long thru the night and were destroyed by the rays of the early morning sun. Papa got a Chinaman by name of Pa On to form a company and plant rice. This was very profitable but finally the land was all drained and planted in cane by my cousin, Hans Faye, for Kekaha Sugar Co., Ltd.

Every year on our annual visits to Niihau there would be new things to do as we grew older and able to take part in the more strenuous sports. We swam and rode our surfboards daily at Nonopapa especially in sheep shearing time. One day in '76, even though we did not go very far out, we were suddenly called in as the natives had seen a shark's fin out beyond the little breakers on which we youngsters were surfing. Cousin Charles Gay, then about sixteen and as expert as an Hawaiian in fishing and swimming, called two of the young native boys to go with him and with long sharp knives swam out to tackle the shark. Just at the right moment when the monster turned over on its back to seize him, Charlie quickly stabbed the shark and killed it. Then he and the boys towed it to shore where an admiring crowd awaited them. It was truly thrilling to see the immense creature beached. Charlie had the jaws with the two rows of moveable teeth hanging in his room at Makaweli for many years.

Several times in the years that followed we stayed at Kawailoa on the eastern end of Niihau where a very comfortable and picturesque grass hut had been built. Fishing off the rocks there and wandering around the base of this volcanic point to find the beautiful spotted cowrie shells clinging to the rocks, was great fun at low tide. This ledge running round the extinct crater, is about thirty feet wide and more or less level, and is quite safe and easy walking. The old natives however warned us to be careful about the tides, and we were told the story of how, when the Sinclair family first came to Niihau, they were caught out on this ledge with the tide coming in. Suddenly a huge wave broke over the ledge carrying little Eliza Gay and Jimmy off their feet. Jimmy grabbed a rock and Uncle Frank caught eight-year old Eliza by her hair! After an hour crowding back against the cliff waiting for the tide to recede they were able to hurry back along the ledge to the hut on the shore of the bay. There they bandaged the little girl's knees which had been terribly torn on the sharp rocks. We used to get her to show us the scars which she carried all her life and beg her to tell us of that thrilling adventure whenever we could persuade her to do so.

One of the most thrilling stories told us as children by Papa was that of the man Kapahee, one of the finest specimens of Hawaiian manhood. He lived on Niihau, and also had *kuleanas*, or holdings, on Kauai, mainly in Kalalau valley, which lies on the north side of Kauai, on the Napali coast. There he had taro patches, and from there he used to take boatloads of taro over to Niiahu, where it does not grow well owing to the scarcity of water, so any shipment was always welcomed on that island.

One day Kapahee started out with a full boatload of taro, a big whale boat it was, and as assistant boatmen he had his wife and one Hawaiian. With sail set, all went well till they reached mid-channel between Mana and Niihau when a sudden squall swept down upon them and capsized the boat, which promptly sank. Seizing an oar, Kapahee gave it to the woman and they struck out for the shore. Being Hawaiians and thoroughly used to the water, they were not disturbed by the fact that they were fifteen miles from the Kauai shore. When, however, they tried to swim to Mana, they found the tide and current so strongly against them that it was impossible to make any headway. Turning their faces southwestward to Niihau and swimming easily they kept together during the afternoon. As night came on and they were still far from land, the man and the woman tired, and Kapahee being the stronger swimmer decided to go on as fast as he could and get help. All night he swam, at first hearing his companions answering *"coo ees"* coming over the ocean, but later as the distance lengthened, their voices were lost in the noise of the wind and the sea. On and on Kapahee's strong arms carried him, and finally in the early dawn he saw he was near the island of Lehua at the north end of Niihau. With difficulty, as he was nearly spent, he made the beach, and pulled himself up on the warm sand. Here he lay for several hours until the sun restored warmth and strength to his thoroughly chilled and exhausted body. As soon as he was able he walked to the end of the little island nearest Niihau, to swim across. This was, he told my father, the hardest part of the whole experience, for it was absolutely abhorrent to him to enter the water again. The thought of his friends behind him gave him strength, and he dived down from a rock and crossed the two miles of ocean to the shore of Niihau. From there he walked several miles to some fishermen's huts, where he had food and clothing given him, and then set out with two canoes to find the swimmers. It is characteristic of the Hawaiian's prowess in the sea to note that they did not fear their friends would have drowned. They felt sure they would be swimming still in the direction Kapahee had taken. But alas, after hours of search through that day and night, and all the next day, in which they were joined by many canoes from along the Niihau coast, no sign was found of the man and the woman. They evidently had succumbed to the chill of the night and the ocean, and had sunk down to a grave on the bed of the sea.

Kapahee lived a long, sturdy, useful life, and was of much use to Papa on Kauai and Uncle Frank on Niihau in regard to all the old landmarks, and the ancient lore of the land. He was the one who told of the huge congregations that gathered at the heiau in Hoea valley just above our home at Waiawa. There would be such a tremendous multitude that when, at a given signal from the *kahunas*, they would shout, the sound could be heard at Hanalei across the mountains! My brother, Augustus, also got many stories of the old religion and laws from Kapahee, which reminded him of Masonic rites.

Grandmama was so devoted to her family she always wanted them near her. She had a way with her that made everyone do what she wished—firm but loving and full of fun, with sympathy in childish doings. She aided and abetted us and we knew she would understand. Even the Hawaiians who called her "Mama" felt that sympathy in her. She was always ministering to them and even when the foolish Hawaiians would come for a dose of *pakai* (salts) then empty the glass round the corner of the house, she would only smile at them knowing their thought was that they wished her to believe they had faith in her medicine. It was most amusing, but finally she persuaded them it was better to be frank and not take the medicine if they only threw it out. She often thought of lovely things to do. I recall a story in connection with Mrs. Rowell, wife of the missionary at Waimea. As Mrs. Rowell told my mother in later years she had been trying to scrape enough money together to send Marion, her clever eldest daughter, to Mt. Holyoke. It seemed quite impossible but one night she prayed God to help her after lying awake trying to form some plans. Finally she fell asleep, waking next morning calm and hopeful. About 9 o'clock a cowboy rode to the gate with a letter from Grandmama, enclosing a large check and saying, "I know there are many things you can use this for and I feel I want to help you." Mrs. Rowell felt it surely was an answer to prayer. Little did Grandmama realize that when Marion returned from college she would become the wife of George Gay, the eldest grandson, and live on Niihau many years.

Both of my parents were interested in the missionaries on Kauai. Mr. Whitney died before my father came to the Islands and Mrs. Whitney lived alone at Waimea where the present Hofgaard home is and still called "Dr. Whitney's Place." She died in December of 1872 when I was but four years and eight months old but I recall that it was a great treat when our father and mother took us to see Mrs. Whitney. She was such a beautiful old lady, hair meticulously dressed and cap and gown fresh and dainty. We were allowed to rummage in her storeroom where we saw piles of cotton print, brown cotton, household supplies, crockery, all sorts of other materials, in fact everything that had been sent out from headquarters in Boston for the "savages." Once a month, Papa would drive in and bring Mrs. Whitney to lunch or rather dinner at noon. She would invariably say, "Oh, Mrs. Knudsen, you have prepared a feast for me." Even our simple meal would seem sumptuous to her who ate so sparingly and usually lived on a baked taro a day with a pint of milk from the Rowells, her neighbors. Once she told Mama of sending her two small sons of 8 and 6 years all the way to her people in New England in the care of a whaling captain and sadly ended her moving story by saying, "That day my heart broke." It seemed imperative, however, that the children be sent away especially those of the isolated families. Another experience Mrs. Whitney told of was one they had about a year after their arrival in Waimea. Two friends from Hanalei had journeyed by canoe as the roads were impassable unless by foot, and

WATERCOLOR PAINTINGS
by
Maud Knudsen Garstin

These watercolors were painted by Maud Knudsen Garstin around the turn of the century. Her granddaughter, Cynthia G. Blackwell, discovered the paintings in Palm Springs, California, after Mrs. Garstin's death in 1948. They had been carefully stored and were in excellent condition.

In April, 1976, the paintings were exhibited at Queen Emma Summer Palace. They are presently on loan to the Kauai Museum, Lihue, Kauai.

MAMA'S FAVORITE WALK
Niihau 1898

WAIAWA RANCH HOUSE
Kauai 1891

WAIAWA TARO PATCH
Kauai 1898

HALEMANU HOUSE
Kokee, Kauai 1891

WAIPO • ABOVE THE FALLS
Kokee, Kauai 1898

WAIMEA CANYON
Kauai 1900

MANA SHORE NEAR BARKING SANDS
Kauai 1898

were to visit the Whitneys for a week. What a joy it was to talk to their own kind and to see their friendly faces and hear English conversation again! For the midday meal Mrs. Whitney had prepared a chicken stew and just as her husband finished grace, in walked the Chiefess of Waimea, fresh from her morning swim with about 20 retainers. All were stark naked except the Princess who had a tapa draped over her shoulders. They all jabbered and laughed pointing at the newcomers, and finally the Chiefess putting her fingers in the stew and fishing out a delicious bit of chicken began to eat it murmuring *"ono maoli."* Finally all departed calling out friendly Alohas to their white teachers. Mama asked, "What did you all do?," to which Mrs. Whitney replied, "We all sat perfectly still with our eyes cast down." I told this story several years ago to a young American friend who was decrying the restraint put upon the Hawaiians by the early missionaries. She declared that if anything similar had happened in her house, she would have called Jack, her husband to "throw them out!" "Yes," I commented, "and start an uprising. With only four white people in the valley and thousands of natives, what chance would they have had and I think they were not only most courageous but possessed of a Godgiven wisdom." My young friend acknowledged she was wrong and said that story gave her a different viewpoint. If only more of the descendants of those fine old missionaries were listened to, the tales one hears from *malihinis* would be silenced. My mother always declared that had it not been for the missionaries no one could have lived in Hawaii as our families did in the middle 1800's. All the work of training and caring for the Hawaiians had begun in 1820 and the loss of the finer traits of the Hawaiians was due to the influence of evil men of all nationalities who came even before the missionaries.

Of Mrs. Whitney's death and funeral, I recall nothing; but the auction held later of all her things made a great impression, especially the auctioneer, young Sam Wilcox, with his black handle-bar mustache and his voice droning on and on. Papa and Mama took us two elder children to the auction and were able to buy some fine old Hawaiian curios and calabashes. Mr. Henry Whitney, her son, was there in charge and other members of her family, but I think my parents felt even more grieved over her death for they enjoyed and loved her always.

On this visit in 1874 after getting us settled on Niihau, my parents left us to meet Aunt Helen, Eliza, Aubrey, Francis and Charles who had gone to Makaweli to join Uncle Hamie and get ready for a trip. The latter had never recovered from an accident in New Zealand in his younger days when a tree had fallen on him, and Mama had finally persuaded Aunt Helen and the others to take him to a specialist in Boston. Quietly he had borne his illness quite unaware of how serious it was, my mother being the only one to see that he was really ill. Just before they were to start he suddenly died at Makaweli, a shock to everyone, especially to Mama, who loved him so deeply. Papa too always spoke of him with high regard and with the greatest affection.

As soon as possible the others started on their journey as the boys needed extra tuition and travel. Papa and Mama joined them and went as far as Salt Lake City, returning then to San Francisco, later touring California and Yosemite Valley. This was all done in large stage coaches and both parents returned to us four months later full of enjoyment of this wonderful trip, of the drives with the coach swaying, the driver cracking his whip and holding his four pairs of horses in absolute control. Mama revelled in it all but a poor woman passenger wrapped her head in a shawl and lay moaning on the floor of the coach. She thought Mama heartless indeed to advise her to "sit up and enjoy the scenery for, if they were to be killed, the view would be a glorious memory to carry to the next world!" Papa also chuckled over an old lady who, when he jumped out at every stop to pick wild flowers for his wife, said with a knowing smile, "It's easy to see you have not been married very long." When he told her they had left four children with their grandmother she could not believe it.

We had been happy and well on Niihau especially as the great tease, Cousin Charlie Gay, had gone to Boston. Uncle Frank had a wonderful time pretending he was our father. Aunt Jean had the real care of us which Uncle Frank and Aunt Isabella shared. The latter was even then working on her *Indigenous Flowers of the Hawaiian Islands* though I do not think she had thought of publishing it then nor until they had shown the paintings to a noted botanist, Sir Joseph Hooker, in London. Aunt Isabella was always full of fun and taught us new games and the Scotch version of "Here we go round the mulberry bush," which runs

> Here we dance looby looby.
> Here we dance looby bright.
> Here we dance looby looby
> All in the pale moonlight.

I recall being fascinated at dancing in the pale moonlight. She told Mama many funny stories of our doings and sayings. One was of Maud being discovered in some childish prank and saying ingratiatingly, "You go away and play the piano, Aunt Bella." Another story was that one day she gave us all a treat of bread and butter with a sprinkling of brown sugar and carraway seeds! As we all went outside to eat our little snack she, peeping through the pantry window, was startled to see Augustus pushing his slice under the house. When she came out and asked him the reason he confided that the bread was "full of wee beasties." Evidently he felt it was wiser to get rid of the treat and the wee beasties at once!

After our return from Niihau another highlight of that year was an invitation from Kanuikino, Papa's overseer at Mana, to christen his new grass house at Polihale. As he was a man of education, taught by the Rev. Mr. Whitney to read and write in his own language, also a man of character and great integrity, Papa was glad to accept the suggestion and off we started in October, I riding on my pet, Prince, and Mama and the nurse and three younger children in the phaeton. Mama asked me to gallop back and tell Papa to bring the coats which had been forgotten on the veranda. As I turned my horse to ride back he gave a sudden jump which unseated me, and dazed by the fall I lay there with Prince holding up his fore foot so as not to injure me. When I finally scrambled out and stood up, to Mama's relief, Papa came galloping up with the little jackets and we all proceeded to Mana, a good two hours' journey. Mama declared she loved Prince from that moment as he had been so quiet and careful not to hurt me.

The never to be forgotten week at picturesque Polihale passed all too quickly. We loved the sweet-smelling new *pili* grass of which the house was built, especially fragrant at night when we thought it a great lark for the whole family to sleep on the big *hikie*. The wonderful cliffs echoing back the roar of the surf, the hunting for ferns and plants and seeing the walled up tombs in the cliffs which Papa told us never to disturb and which he himself held sacred to the memory of departed Hawaiians. He told of the belief of the Hawaiians that those cliffs were the place from where the souls of the dead descended to *Po* in the ocean depths. Papa also pointed out that in this new grass house Kanuikino had the doors opening east and west which was planned to keep the souls from going through the house as the ancient lore declared they did on their way to the Polihale cliffs! We found maiden hair ferns growing in a cave along the rocky beach where fresh water dripped down, and saw the spring of pure water running out from under the cliffs, obtainable only at low tide when its exit was marked by the bright green limu or moss. Our old Hawaiian host came to see us several times from his house in Mana village just mauka and east of the *Nohili* or sounding sands. He was evidently touched by the kindness of the *haku* (master) and declared then and later that the visit of Kanuka, Annie and the *keikis* had brought him good luck.

The following June in 1875 my youngest brother, Arthur Sinclair, was born and, as usual, was taken to Niihau to be shown to Grandmama. We did not stay long, as having missed Halemanu the year before, Mama and Papa were keen to take us all up there in the late summer. The return trip from Niihau was made in the old *S.S. Kilauea* which anchored very far out from Kii as the captain was not familiar with that shore and so-called landing. Our whale boat crew manfully pulled us all out only to find the swells so huge we could not board the steamer by the usual way, so the captain ordered the hold opened, whereupon a *kanaka* grabbed baby Arther and swung him towards the men in the hold. It gave poor Mama a terrible shock to see her wee baby thrown through the air from one man to another but when she saw he was safe, she let us all be swung over. Finally, two men managed to hoist her and Papa on board, the steamer heaving and pitching all the while. The crossing to Waimea was a short one but oh so terribly rough, and night had closed in before we reached dear peaceful Waiawa.

Halemanu was of course our favorite haunt above all other places. We could easily walk to the canyon to admire the wild beauty and brilliant colors of the cliffs, and it was here we always went on Sundays after supper to sing hymns with great gusto. We knew many of the Moody and Sankey hymns, one especially seemed appropriate with its stirring tune, one line of which, "Sound the proclamation over dale and hill," comes to my mind. Papa brought us little hatchets and he and Mama taught us to chop away bushes and big ferns and to make roads. The first one was to the canyon view, the next up to the head of our little stream "Nawaimaka," which water bubbled out of a sort of underground cave only ten minutes' walk from the camp. Later we engineered a road to Waipo, and also up on the hill looking down into Kumuwela where once we saw cattle browsing in the valley below. Charlie Storrbach, who was a splendid shot, was with us, and Papa sent him to shoot one of the young animals. While we kept very still he crept down near the herd and managed to shoot one, which supplied us all with fresh meat, but what especially thrilled us was to be in at the death! These wild cattle were descendants of Papa's first herd which he bought from Mr. Wyllie. A few had escaped into the mountains where, owing to the dense forests and jungles, they could not be driven out. We could hear them bellowing at night and see them sometimes on our horseback trips when, alarmed at seeing people, they crashed their way through the woods. In later years my brothers had many a wild hunt and I recall hearing Charlie Storrbach tell of an awful encounter with one of these immense wild bulls. It had fallen with Charlie's two well aimed shots but as he was looking at his prize lying "dead" on the ground, the bull suddenly revived and, lunging at Charlie, pinned him to the trunk of a huge lehua tree. Fortunately its two long sharp horns went on each side of his body but the glaring eyes and awful hot breath of the bull made Charlie feel his last hour had come. Finally, with a last roar and dying gasp, the creature fell over and died, leaving Charlie absolutely shaken and weak. Mama had noticed when he returned to Waiawa the next day with the hide, head and horns, how pale and strained he looked, and prompted by her sympathetic questioning he told us the story of this dreadful experience.

 I remember once when some one asked Mama how she could bear to have her children running along the cliffs of the Waimea Canyon, hunting wild cattle, exploring the Alakai Swamp, etc. she replied, "If they are so fool-hardy as to fall over, or become lost, I tell them it will be good riddance to bad rubbish."

 While in California in 1874 Papa had invited his favorite nephew, Alexander Seippel of Oslo, Norway, who was taking a post graduate course at Harvard, to join them in San Francisco. He enjoyed the experience of seeing the West and of meeting his Uncle and Aunt again. He sent back to me by my mother a tiny white-handled knife, a gift I treasured for many years and for which Mama made little pockets in all my dresses with a flap which buttoned down. The summer after their return this wee knife played a telling part in an adventure we had with our father. One late afternoon he came in from a long days' tramp over the Alakai swamp and was thrilled when he told Mama he had found the fly-catching plant. We all crowded around as he unpacked his collector's tin and showed us the tiny plant with one leaf curled over and feeding on or absorbing a fly. Immediately after supper he set about pressing the valuable specimen. Suddenly all were startled to hear a strange sound like the ringing chop of an axe. Exclaiming, "There is something wrong with the horses," Papa ran out to the natives' houses where he begged the cowboys to follow him. "Oh, no" they answered, "That's the *Akua* chopping wood and we must not disturb him." Disgusted with their superstition Papa turned up the trail, Augustus and I scurrying after him like rabbits. To our horror and dismay, we found one of the horses had fallen over a log and was gasping his life away with the lariat taut around his neck. Papa felt in his pocket for his knife but to his consternation found he had left it on the table when trimming his ferns. At this moment I said "Papa, I have my little knife." I drew it out of my pocket and Papa opened the blade and cut through the rope, relieving the poor horse which rolled over with a groan. Next day we saw the horse wandering about and eating a little, but its neck was still very swollen. When Papa joked the cowboys about the *"akua* chopping wood" Punoalii, whose horse it was, looked quite sheepish, but Makaawaawa, the cook, still maintained that it was the *akua*, and it was only incidental that Papa found the horse in trouble! I was quite proud when Papa declared I was the real savior, for had I not had my little knife safely in my pocket the horse would have choked to death. I kept my little knife for several years, only losing it when it slipped down between the wide cracks of the attic flooring in the old barn we called the Long House. Papa would not be bothered to take up the flooring as I timidly suggested, so there lay my wee knife entombed. Over forty years later the old house was pulled down but I was not there to see if my knife could be found and doubtless after so many years it had rusted away.

We stayed late into October at Halemanu as the weather was glorious but on the day set for our return the cowboys arrived in rain with reports that a Kona storm was brewing. After a consultation our parents decided to start down at once as a Kona storm usually lasted three weeks and the roads would become impassable. Augustus and I were put on our horses in the pouring rain, Mama converting red blankets into storm capes. Put on over our heads, tied round the necks and hanging down over our knees like a poncho, the blankets kept us very dry and we were told by Papa to let our horses find their own way down the steep trails following the men who were carrying Maud and Eric.

The memory of that ride down the slippery road to the flooded Halemanu stream thru which our horses floundered, and then up the equally steep and difficult ridge trail to the top was truly frightening and will never be forgotten. However, we obeyed Papa and remembered his admonition as we started, "Sit still, hold on tight, and let your horse do it all!"

Maka-e, our faithful nurse, would not allow anyone to take Baby Arthur, but walked carrying him wrapped in a shawl with an umbrella over their heads. She waded the swollen stream and climbed the steep mountain trail towards Puu ka Pele. The storm was then lifting and she waited to give the baby to Mama who rode up on her horse. Then the cook, her husband, with his little boy of five and carrying his baby girl of two years, joined Maka-e and they took the road at the fork which led to the village of Poki. The little girl had not been named. Mama had suggested several which however were politely ignored. Next morning when the cook and Maka-e came they announced happily that the child had been named. It was "Kailianu" little "cold skin," so appropriately named by her small brother as the poor child had become very wet and cold on the long ride. Mama was secretly disgusted but, of course, openly rejoiced for a name had finally been found for the wee girl.

As we grew out of babyhood and could ride well we spent every summer from June to September in the mountains. It was a grand thing for us children to get away from the heat of the lowlands and to make us hardy and clever in mountain life. We could saddle and care for our horses and never were frightened to go after Papa on the most slippery trails or break through the ferns and underbrush on exploring a new path even though our horses often would leap over huge logs which came nearly up to their bellies. One year Papa had men come to see if a road could be engineered over the Kalalau ridge as he thought from some of the old legends that it might be possible, and in that way escape the crossing of the treacherous Alakai Swamp. Several times Augustus and I accompanied him and one day while climbing ahead through the low foliage and lehua trees I came upon a lovely view of the west and down thousands of feet. I called Papa who was much excited, especially after the natives told him it was Kalalau Valley. Next day after telling Mama about it, she came up with us and was also thrilled at my discovery and when Papa named the little peak "Puu Ita" after me I was very proud. Later a road was cut to a better place to have picnics and to see the view of the valley. There are two little stone figures on the ridge which, according to native lore, are two of the *akua's* children who had been down to the beach. They had been fishing and playing with human children until there was not time to reach the mountain home of the *akuas* up in the mists before the sun touched them and turned them into stone!

On our way home we rode down a different way, very rough and deeply eroded. Suddenly old Stirling, Mama's horse named for her birthplace in Scotland, and who had been given to me, slipped his left hind leg through a tough lehua root on the upper edge of a "jump down" of at least three feet. In trying to extricate his leg he heaved and plunged while I was thrown down on to his neck until I was finally clinging to his ears when the cowboy reached my side and helped me off. After a little more heaving the root broke and though the poor old horse's upper hind leg was cruelly bruised and bleeding, he carried me safely back without even a limp.

Early in '76 when Grandmama was still on Niihau, Uncle Frank was busy at Makaweli making a new road. He came down to Waiawa and invited us all up there for a visit. As my father was at the Legislature in Honolulu, Mama thought it a fine plan to keep Uncle Frank company and give us all a change. It was an adventurous journey, Uncle Frank and a cowboy riding in front, then Mama driving the phaeton, and several Hawaiians behind leading a pack horse and our saddle horses. We had passed through Poki and Kekaha and were on the Waimea road when one back wheel fell off and we bumped along several yards before old Hikili could be stopped. Augustus, Maud and I were sitting on the little front seat and were all thrown at Mother's feet. Uncle Frank soon rode back and with the Hawaiians found the pin which was quickly adjusted and as soon as the wheel was in place, off we started again, Uncle Frank laughing heartily as he heard Mama saying when putting us back on the right seat, "Sit still and keep your mouths shut or you'll bite your tongues off." A half hour later we came to the bank of the Waimea River only to find the scow out of order. However, we were soon mounted on our horses and two *paniolas* carried Eric and Arthur, less than a year old. Piloted by Uncle Frank, we rode down to the mouth of the river where we were warned to ride close behind him where the surf ripples and the stream met, and in that manner escape the quicksands which were often found near the wide river's mouth. One daring young half-grown Hawaiian boy however rode his horse into the river about twenty-five feet above our party and to our dismay the horse began sinking in the quicksand. The other native boys who had already crossed safely in front of our party lassoed the boy and pulled him out. The poor frightened horse by that time was down so deep we could just see the upper part of its back and its head and neck. It took the combined strength of three horses and men to finally pull the poor animal out and the boy surely deserved the good scolding Uncle Frank gave him.

Our stay at Makaweli House that year was the first that I can remember. How we loved Uncle Frank's stories of the *menehunes* at Pupu Kaniau where they guarded the cool sparkling water which in earlier days had been carried down the mountain side swiftly to the king at Waimea. As at Halemanu, lovely birds by the hundred flitted about and sang and our three weeks passed all too quickly. After Aunt Helen's return from Boston, Grandmama made Makaweli her home with Aunt Helen, Aunt Jean, Aubrey, Francis, Charles, Eliza and Alice and a tutor for the boys.

Isabella Bird, the authoress, came on a tour of Kauai and spent the greater part of her time at Makaweli with the Sinclair Clan. She was an extraordinary looking woman as I remember her on her visit to Waiawa, wearing the first "bloomers" to be seen in the islands. It was an odd looking garment, very full and tied at the ankles, which with an old hat and her high color and very prominent teeth made her look anything but prepossessing. My parents enjoyed her company as she was clever and well read and had traveled extensively. Her description of my grandmother and the family at Makaweli House in her book "Six Months in the Sandwich Islands," is, I think, quite delightful. To quote: "The household here consists first and foremost of its Head, Mrs. Francis Sinclair, a lady of the old Scotch type, very talented, bright, charming, with a definite character which impresses its force on everyone. Beautiful in her old age, disdaining that senile conformity to prevailing fashion which makes many old people at once ugly and contemptible, speaking with a slight oldfashioned and refined Scotch accent which gives naiveté to everything she says, up to the latest novelty in theology or politics, devoted to her children and grandchildren, the life of the family and tho upwards of seventy [she was then over seventy-four] the first to rise and the last to retire in the house! She was away when I came but some days afterwards she rode up on horseback in a large drawn silk bonnet which she rarely lays aside, as light in her figure and step as a young girl and looking as if she had walked out of an old picture or one of Dean Ramsay's books." This picture coincides with my memory of my grandmother and reminds me of a story told of her when over eighty. A pleasant gentleman had been a guest for two days and while thanking her for her hospitality asked if he might know her age. She replied, "But you must know ladies do not like to tell their age." He agreed but said he felt that after a certain age they did not mind. "Oh well," retorted Grandmama, "I have not reached that certain age yet," and with that the gentleman was defeated and quickly departed.

Tho I could read quite fluently at six years, when I was $7\frac{1}{2}$, the time had come for regular schooling. During the forenoon our mother gave us reading, writing and music lessons from 9 to 11. Then Papa would come in from his work and give us arithmetic and German and also taught us a number of German and Norwegian folk songs. Of the latter I can remember several of his favorites, "Borjig, paa det höja Fjeld" and "O, Kjöre Vatten o Kjöre Ve." Maud, tho only five and a half years old, sang very well and one day was called upon by Papa to sing "Borjeg paa det Höja Fjeld" to Dr. Smith, who was over on one of his government medical inspections. She hopped up on a little stool and looking at Dr. Smith, evidently thought the rollicking mountain song would be inappropriate so began very solemnly, "The Lord is my Shepherd, I Shall Not Want." Mama had been teaching us the grand old psalm to sing on Sundays and Maud's hunch and rendition of it to the old Doctor and clergyman almost convulsed both our parents. However, they made no comment, finally persuading her a little later to sing the Norske song. I've no doubt Dr. Smith enjoyed the whole show as he always had a merry twinkle in his eye.

Mama began to teach me to sew and to help her with the cooking. I soon could churn the butter, the cream having been hung out all night in a stone jar set in a bucket of water where the cool night breeze blew down from the mountains. Later I always boiled the eggs for breakfast as our Hawaiian cooks invariably served them hard boiled just as they never failed to churn the cream so fast it would become whipped cream. Being an early bird, always up by five o'clock, it was easy for me to do it and when I was twelve and we got ice weekly from Honolulu I could make the butter in a bowl in a very short time. The first time I saw ice was in Honolulu when I was ten years old! When I was twelve years old I set the *hu* (yeast loaf), kneaded it next morning and put it in bread pans to rise by the stove, then baked it and took one loaf to my father to sample. He was sitting out on the veranda on the oldfashioned koa settee now at Kikila. Was I proud as he cut the *skalk* (Norwegian for crust), buttered it and nodding his head at the first taste said, "Pretty good for my little girl."

At Waiawa there was the best of simple food. A young steer was butchered once a month and a sheep which gave us fresh meat every two weeks. Of course we had chickens, fish and eggs and occasionally a turkey to vary our diet. Mama was an expert at "corning" beef and also made the most delicious mutton hams after a Norwegian recipe and I shall never forget the *söde suppe* (sweet fruit soup) and the *rödgröd* which she made for us. She and Papa were marvelous gardeners and we always had vegetables. Taro, white and mealy from Poki, the yellow sweet potatoe, *hua moa*, from Mana, and oh such delicious watermelons, both red and yellow with black seeds. We used the taro leaves for spinach and the stalks called *Ha ha* for asparagus, also a spinach of young sweet potatoe leaves made a nice change. We all had little watering pots and after our five o'clock

Anne Sinclair Knudsen
1909
Bishop Museum Photo

supper when the servants went home to the village, we helped to keep all the flowers and vegetables watered. Then we would sit on the steps in the gloaming while our parents told us stories of their young days, or gave us talks on strange lands or sagas, the names of stars and constellations and much else of scientific lore. When we were quite small I remember my father taking us to the mauka veranda at Waiawa where we could see a wonderful display of lightning up on the high mountains and hear the thunder reverberating from hill to hill as he explained the cause and encouraged us never to be afraid.

We had lessons in botany and were taught how to collect ferns and flowers in our little tin collector's cans, especially when at Halemanu. Learning the names of the many beautiful specimens found on our long walks, also of the trees and birds was fascinating. We were encouraged to choose favorite ferns, mine being the *Davalia Tennfolia* and Maud's the *Dodia Media*, but we knew many others, the *Douglassi*, the different *Hillibrandis*, the *Adiantum neg*, etc.

Even though Papa was stern and both parents exacted the utmost obedience, our only punishment was being "put in the corner," which we felt was a terrible disgrace. They were, however, full of fun, teaching us all sorts of games— to act charades, and to sing and recite, and also stimulating a love of adventure. In all these ways the life at Waiawa went on leaving its impressions in those early years and developing a love for art, music, literature and science and a devotion to religion expressed in many ways, but especially in a short service every Sunday forenoon whether at home or up in the mountains and even while we were in New Zealand or abroad.

Giving to their children everything that two clever, cultivated and deeply spiritual people could in this intimate and unforgettable manner, our parents drew us into a very close bond of love and happy association which influenced us all our lives.

CHAPTER VI

The Anglo-Germanic Alliance

IN ENGLAND, at Upton-cum-Charvey on July 27, 1804, Thomas Brown was born. He studied landscape gardening, finally becoming partner in the famous gardens at Slough, near Windsor. He was often called by the superintendent of the Windsor Castle gardens for consultation and advice, and later Queen Victoria commanded him to take charge of all the gardens and hot houses. He used his gift of landscape gardening in laying out further beautiful vistas through the wide expanses of the castle, whose parks and gardens had been sadly neglected during the reign of the Georges.

On October 15, 1836, Thomas Brown married Mary Ann Rhodes, born at Stepney, July 11, 1813, the daughter of Godfrey Rhodes, an official of the Bank of England, and grand-daughter of Monsieur and Madame du Collier, descendants of the Huguenots who had fled from France at the time of the persecution of that sect. Many came to England, also crossed the sea to Novia Scotia and America. Longfellow's poem, "Evangeline," is based on the flight of some of these Huguenots to Arcadia in Nova Scotia.

It was before and during the early years of Victoria's reign that the craze for tulips from Holland was in vogue, and Thomas Brown was instrumental in growing some of the rarest for Her Majesty. In the family heirloom, "the painting of the three tulips," Windsor Castle is shown in the background, as it appeared from the Brown home in nearby Slough. This painting is by Bristow, and the prize awarded for the tulips was a silver punch ladle still in the possession of the family. The family home was surrounded by lovely gardens and hot houses, and over it grew a famous large wisteria vine, known far and wide through England, and still growing as late as 1921 when my husband and I, accompanied by Hilda, Ronald, and Katharine, visited there on our motor trip through England.

The Browns, living at Slough, had three sons, Arthur, Frank, and Godfrey, and on June 4, 1840, a daughter, Alice, was born amid great rejoicing. Several years later Thomas Brown's health began to fail, and his physician recommended a change to a warmer climate. Mrs. Brown's brothers, Henry Rhodes in Victoria, and Godfrey Rhodes in Hawaii, had both written glowing accounts of the climate and opportunities in the new countries, so the Browns left England sometime in 1845 in a sailing ship, and went first to New York, thence to Buenos Aires, and then around the Horn to Honolulu. What courage it must have taken to start out with four children all under ten years old, on the long six months' voyage! But all went well, and the invalid's health was restored before the journey's end. Mr. Brown had had installed on the deck of the vessel several hot houses, with many plants which he visioned as beautifying their new home and country. Among the ones I remember being told of were: three magnolias, one of which is still alive and blossoming at Hanalei, Kauai; the Duranta, Tacoma Japonica vine, Virgin or Easter lily, passion vine, and wisteria.

When the party arrived in Honolulu they were met by Godfrey Rhodes, and a Mr. Dudoit, and stayed at the latter's home for some time, where Alice formed a fast friendship with Julia Dudoit, who was about the same age. A new venture, a coffee plantation on Kauai, was being talked of, in which Godfrey Rhodes was financially interested, and which appealed to Mr. Brown. So to Kauai they went, where a home was built, called Waialua Falls Mansion, commanding a glorious view of the falls, river, and surrounding country. This house had been designed and cut in England, and brought out on the sailing vessel, and in-

Thomas Brown
1804–1886

Mary Ann Rhodes Brown
1813–1900

cluded a secret room to hide in, in case of an "attack by savages." Before coming to the islands Mrs. Brown had been told that the native servants always called their masters and mistresses by their first names. She was determined not to be thus familiarly addressed, so she told Mr. Brown never to call her Mary Ann in front of the servants. He dutifully complied. What was her consternation after a few days to have her large Hawaiian cook appear and ask her in front of her guests, "My love, what time do you want me to serve dinner?"

At Waialua Falls Mansion, Cecil, Malcolm, and Louis were born, the latter dying in infancy; and there several years were happily spent. To the hospitable home many a traveler came, and as the road leading to the house could be seen for many miles, Mrs. Brown always prepared some refreshing drink for her coming guests. On one occasion when she recognized a reverend gentleman approaching, she prepared a glass of milk with sherry wine and set it in the spring house to cool. When the visitor had been made welcome and had refused, as she knew he would, any spirituous refreshment, she led him to the spring house and offered him the glass of milk! He drained it to the last drop, and then remarked, "Mrs. Brown, WHAT a cow!" She was a dear, lovely person, always full of good deeds, and often her strength was overtaxed with her large family and poor servants, but they all loved Kauai. One sad story of this time was the death of Julia Dudoit, Alice's friend who had come for a visit with her mother. The two girls were bathing in the river when a sudden freshet swept them away. An old Hawaiian came to their rescue, pulled Alice out of the swirling water by her long hair and, placing her on the hot rocks by the side of the stream, went back for Julia. But alas, it was too late and the little girl did not revive.

After a few years the coffee trees all died, due to the fact that the roots struck a layer of sea sand, forcing the abandonment of the plantation. Mr. Brown then started a cattle ranch, at which the three older boys soon became adept, but this too was not successful, and as the family wished to give the children opportunities for higher education, they left for New York, their second trip around the Horn. Arthur took to the sea, and had his own ship. He married a lovely girl, Rose French, but unfortunately died of yellow fever while on a trip to the West Indies. Godfrey and Frank took a business course, while Cecil studied law. The family then returned to Honolulu, where they were established in a home on School St. near Queen Emma St., called "Kahihuna." Mr. Brown was appointed Recorder of Deeds by Kamehameha IV, a position which he held for thirty years.

When Alice was about sixteen years old, she and Malcolm went with Mr. and Mrs. Brown on a fast American clipper ship for another trip to New York, with a few other passengers aboard. When off the coast of South America they were fired on by a French frigate which was looking for pirates, but on displaying the American flag, the frigate withdrew. This was quite exciting to Alice.

Good winds were behind them all the way, so strong that they went around the Horn in one night instead of the usual two or three days, and it continued so strong that they were blown off their course and too close to land, so that they struck a sand bar off the coast of Brazil near Santos, and were unable to save the ship.

Salvaging food, arms, and some clothing, the passengers and crew made camp on the beach and began their plans for locating inland trails hoping to find help. Mrs. Brown, because of her knowledge of French, accompanied the searching party, as the native Portuguese understood that language. Heading north the group was fortunate to encounter a caravan of Portuguese gentlemen after only two days' journey. They were en route from Sao Paulo to Rio de Janeiro, and carried the message of distress to the American consul at the latter city. He soon dispatched a vessel to the rescue of the marooned group, who in the meantime had had quite a distressing time. It seems that several casks of liquor, which were part of the cargo of the wrecked vessel, had drifted ashore as it broke up under the pounding of the waves, and the crew indulged much too freely and threatened the captain and passengers. The captain barricaded the party behind the ship's stores, armed them all, including young Alice, and they spent a sleepless night, but all was well as soon as the effects of the spree had worn off. The whole company were most grateful to be on their way to New York again. The return trip to Honolulu was the fifth trip made around the Horn by the Browns, which must be some sort of a record.

Godfrey and Cecil held positions of trust in the Honolulu community, Godfrey being Minister of Finance to the King and one of the founders of the Hawaiian Electric Company and of the Mutual Telephone Company. Cecil served as Senator for a number of terms in the Legislature and was the first president of the First National Bank of Honolulu, which is now the Bishop National Bank.

Alice, called Lily by the family, was a most lovable young girl and had many warm friends and admirers. Young Hermann von Holt was among these. He arrived from Hamburg, Germany, in 1858, being out of sympathy with the Prussian government, and, in 1861, established a mercantile business under the name of "von Holt & Heuck." He was the son of Christopher and Marie Martens von Holt, and had two brothers and a sister living in Hamburg: Alexander, Thomas Heinrich, and Bertha.

In 1862 the young Hanoverian won the hand of the fair Lily, and they were married in October. The following item appeared in the weekly paper *The Polynesian* of October 18th. "One by one the lilies are gathered in the bridal wreath, and of late marriage has followed marriage in quick succession. May happiness and sunshine wait on them all. On Wednesday last Mr. Hermann von Holt, Hanoverian Consul, led to the altar Miss Alice Brown, daughter of Thomas Brown of this city. The marriage ceremony was performed after the English Episcopalian rite at the Bethel Church by the Rev. S. Damon. The ladies and gentlemen

Alice Brown and Hermann von Holt
1862
Bishop Museum Photo

who assisted on the occassion were Miss Jenny McKibbin and Mr. Ernest Krull, Miss Fanny Corney and Mr. Charles Hart, Miss Blanche Dudoit and Mr. F. Banning, and Miss Ida von Pfister and Mr. Alexander McKibbin."

The little paper was of one sheet only, and spoke of the arrival of the English Mission headed by Bishop Staley, described the presents sent out by them from Queen Victoria to the King and Queen and the little Prince, and gave quite a long account of a presentation of a silver salver to Mr. Damon, which followed the marriage of the von Holts. This was given to him "in token of respect, esteem, and affection, from the ladies and gentlemen of the Episcopal faith who have been regularly attendant on his religious ministrations. The presentation was made by His Excellency R. C. Wyllie and Miss Mary Luce."

Lily Brown had been a faithful member of Mr. Damon's Bethel Church, had sung in the choir and taught in the Sunday School, but as Bishop Staley had come to establish the Episcopal Church, she and the other English people of the community were of course to join him.

The young couple lived at Sunnyslope on the hill on Nuuanu Avenue. This house was cut in Boston, shipped to China, and finally came back to Honolulu where Mr. von Holt bought it. Here were born their three children, Harry Martens on September 15, 1863, Marie Rosalie on February 12, 1865, and Bertha Louise on February 7, 1866. It was a tragic day for this happy family when, a year later, young Mr. von Holt was thrown from his horse and seriously injured in the head. He was riding among the taro patches in Pauoa Valley with a party of friends when one of them suddenly slapped his horse on the rump. The horse naturally jumped, and unseated his rider. He soon remounted, but on returning home was quite nauseated and upset, and several weeks later began to have terrible cramps in his legs, and had to go to the hospital. No one in those days knew of trepanning the skull, and the only recommendation was that he take a long sea voyage back to Germany and see

Alice Brown von Holt with Harry
1864
Bishop Museum Photo

Margaretha Martens
1828

Johann Hinrich Martens
1828

what the doctors there could do for him. The poor little wife, with her three small babies could not accompany him, so went to live with her parents at Kahihuna. Sustained with their love, and by her own calm and beautiful spirit, she managed to keep cheerful. After many months the ship returned, and the captain told the sad details of the death of Hermann J. F. von Holt, and of his burial at sea, when about half way across the Atlantic. At first the voyage had benefitted him, said the captain, but one day when the German captain came to his cabin, Mr. von Holt said in English, "I cannot speak nor understand my mother tongue, and beg of you to speak to me in English." After giving the captain a few messages for his wife and little family, and for his brothers Heinrich and Alexander and sister Bertha in Hamburg, he lapsed into unconsciousness and died.

Harry von Holt, baptised Hinrich Martens after his maternal great-grandfather, was with his mother and grandparents at Waikiki, and remembered clearly his mother's weeping at the sad tidings. Harry, tho not five years old, remembered much about his father, and many of the stories he told about his young life in Germany. When he and I went to Germany in 1901 we went with the aunt and uncles to the Stammschloss von Holt in Obensdorf, a two hours' railway trip from Hamburg, to have lunch with the owner, a cousin Wilhelm von Holt. I remember that he and his wife and young people were most enthusiastic over my being able to speak German to them. When Harry had visited them in 1889 he had astonished all the relatives with his knowledge of the family and estates in Obensdorf. The land had been granted to a certain Baron Holten by Gustavus Adolphus when he came down from Sweden in 1830 and conquered all the north German country. Baron Holten was Swedish, but established himself in Obensdorf, and as a generation or two passed, the name changed to the German form von Holt. In the 16th and 17th centuries the "en" at the end of a name denoted "of." Holten was "of Holt" in the Scandinavian countries, while in Germany "von Holt" denoted "of Holt." Over the door of the old house was an inscription as follows:

Gott bewahre dieses Haus und de Einwohner
Den Ein und Ausgang mein, lass Dir O Gott, befohlen sein.

Peter Rape	19 Aug. Anno 1671
Thomas	Katharine
von Holten	von Holten
Anno	1766, den 26 Mai

It is thought that Peter Rape was the original owner of the house, and that Thomas and Katharine added their names to the carved motto when they bought it. The translation runs thus: "God protect this house and the dwellers therein. My incoming and outgoing be in Thy hands, O God." Marie made a faithful replica of this inscription which hung in the front hall of Palikea for many years.

On this visit in 1901 we brought Mary and Hermann, our eldest son, named, as was the von Holt custom, after his grandfather. In talking of the remaining children at home we told of Hilda, Ronald and Katharine. At mention of the last, Cousin Wilhelm asked, "Why did you choose Katharine? It is not a family name," whereupon Harry led him out to the old house in the back, and pointing to the inscription over the door, convinced him that we had certainly chosen a family name!

In 1910 when Harry and I again visited Germany, he went with Marie and his niece Constance Glade to Hanover to see the monument to the men who fell in the battle of Waterloo. On the back of this imposing column they found the name of "Thomas v. Holt, Ober Fahner Viertes oder Landwehr Bataillon Bremervorde." Harry also met a Mr. Valdemar von Holten who was of the same family and who wanted Harry to take the old name von Holten again. This gentleman showed Harry a family tree that he was working on, which traced the family as far back as "Claus von Holten, Landsmann im Obendorf am Oster" and who had died before 1669.

Alice Mackintosh with Children
Bertha, Marie, Harry von Holt
Alexander St. Martin, Aeneas Ramsay,
Cecil Arthur Mackintosh
Alice Brown von Holt Mackintosh
1883
Bishop Museum Photo

Papa Hermann, as his children called him, left property on King St. now called the von Holt Block, where Harry built a fine business block rented for years to Dimond & Co. Later, on their amalgamation with E. O. Hall & Son, the building was renovated and changed to a movie theatre called the King Theatre. The home Papa Hermann had so loved, Sunnyslope, was now the center of the family life, as Grandpapa and Grandmama Brown and their son Malcolm came to live with the von Holt children and their mother. This young uncle was a great tease, and one day when it was Harry's turn to say grace he electrified them all by saying quite reverently, "Please God, make dead Mally," evidently sure his Heavenly Father would come to his rescue and rid him of the tease. Another story of Harry was that when reproved for spitting over the veranda railing he calmly remarked, "I'm 'moking, and when I 'mokes, I 'pits." Evidently he had both a vivid imagination and trouble with his sibilants!

When Harry was nine years old, in 1873, his mother, whom the children called Mutter Lily, as their father had taught them, married the Reverend Alexander Mackintosh, a young clergyman sent out from England by the Society for the Propagation of the Gospel, to assist Bishop Staley. He was first cousin of the Chief of Clan Chattan, the Mackintosh of Mackintosh, and a very charming and well read young man, very popular with all, and much in favor with Lily's parents. A wing was added to Sunnyslope with two rooms upstairs for Grandpapa and Grandmama Brown, and a bedroom, bath and study downstairs for the bride and groom.

A year later when Harry was ten, his first step-brother, Alexander St. Martin Mackintosh, was born. In two years Aeneas Ramsay arrived, and finally Cecil Arthur in 1879. Harry, Marie, and Bertha each claimed one of the little brothers as their special care, and it was certainly a happy busy family. Mr. Mackintosh was an unusually good teacher, and gave much to his children and step-children, who

Family Group at Sunnyslope
1895
Front row l to r: Ida von Holt and Mary, Marie von Holt,
Constance and Alice Glade, Mrs. Thomas Brown,
Mrs. Alexander Mackintosh
Back Row l to r: Harry von Holt with Herman,
The Reverend Alexander Mackintosh, Bertha von Holt Glade,
A. St. Martin Mackintosh
Bishop Museum Photo

all called him Daddy. He was for many years principal of the Royal School and a great number of the prominent men and women of the city and the islands owe their early training to him. He was Royal Chaplain to King Kamehameha IV and Queen Emma, and later had the honor of placing the crown on the head of King Kalakaua when that monarch had his elaborate coronation.

He did not care for the name of Lily, so the children began to call their mother "Mammy," and later when they all towered above her, "Little Mammy." He always spoke of her as Alice and had many endearing names for her. I can remember him laughing one day and saying "Oh, you essence of delight!"

One day Arthur, when only three years old, was lost, and riding parties were out searching for him. St. Martin, who was about six, looked up at his mother and told her not to worry, as he had just "seen" Arthur being picked up by Uncle Mally at the corner of School St. and they were all riding up Nuuanu. Sure enough, in about ten minutes the riders appeared with Arthur safe and sound and everything exactly as St. Martin had described it, a clear case of second sight!

Both the Mackintoshes and the Browns loved entertaining in a quiet way, and were often hosts to all sorts of waifs and strays as well as their friends. Queen Emma was a frequent visitor and later Queen Kapiolani often drove up from the palace before breakfast to consult with Mrs. Mackintosh about the affairs of the Kapiolani Maternity Hospital, of which they were both trustees. The Hospital Flower Society, which has grown into the present Social Service department of Queen's Hospital, was founded by Mrs. Mackintosh, and she was also a charter member of the Stranger's Friend Society. King Kalakaua came frequently to help Mr. Mackintosh with his Hawaiian sermons, and there were visits from Princess Likelike and her husband, the Honorable A. S. Cleghorn. Princess Kaiulani, their daughter, rode up many times, from Ainahau, to spend the day with the girls, reading fairy stories, which she adored, and singing and playing the piano.

My sister Marie tells me the following story of a voyage to Oregon from Honolulu:

"In the year 1882 it was decided that Bertha and I should have a change of climate and environment. We were growing up to think that Hawaii was the only place in the world, we were forming unfavorable attachments, and our parents thought we needed to broaden our outlook on life. After correspondence with friends in Oregon and California it was decided that we should be sent to St. Helen's Hall in Portland, Oregon.

"At this time the iron bark *Ulloch* came to port in ballast from Liverpool, consigned to T. H. Davies and Co. The ship was bound to Portland to fill up with wheat as return cargo, so the agents graciously allowed us a passage though it was not fitted for passengers. My brother Harry had previously been to Portland on the *Mattie Macleay* with our parents, to attend the Bishop Scott Academy there, so he accompanied us as he 'knew the ropes.'

"We left in March, and it must have been on a Thursday morning, because in those good old days all our friends set aside Wednesday evening at the Fort St. Church for Prayer Meeting, and we in the Cathedral had Evensong and choir practice afterwards. On the evening previous to our departure the Psalm contained the words, 'How shall we sing the Lord's song in a strange land?' Bertha and I broke down and wept, and the congregation wept too, as Honolulu was a small place and we knew everyone, and everyone knew of our coming adventure.

"We took everything we owned on board in large trunks. I remember a large picture of Rosa Bonheur's 'Three Horses' and many pen and ink sketches which we hung in our room at school. We collected all the old clothes we could find, and threw them overboard when they were soiled, as there was no chance to do any laundry while on board.

"The passage took us twenty-five days, but out of these twenty-five days we actually sailed only fifteen, the rest of the time we were becalmed, tossing in huge troughs, and having to be tied in our chairs on the deck. Bertha and I shared one small cabin with only one bunk. One of us slept at the head and one at the foot, so it was lucky we were young and strong. To reach the bunk we had to put one foot on the wash stand, and then leap, hoping to reach the berth safely! We both had very long hair, and to get it properly brushed we had to open our door and brush first one side out into the saloon and then turn and brush the other. Harry had a bunk opposite ours in the saloon and his berth was so narrow that he could not turn over, but had to get out, turn, and get 'interned' again!

"We arrived in Puget Sound in a very heavy fog, and had to land at a small place quite far from Portland, being rowed ashore in the ship's boats, but people were kind to us and sent us on our way to stay with friends in the city. Our first Sunday the same psalm was sung that we had practiced in the choir at home, 'By the waters of Babylon we sat down and wept', so we felt quite at home, and I do not remember that we were homesick at all during our school days."

After the completion of their education in Oregon, the young von Holts entered the social life of Honolulu. Many were the balls and levees at the Palace where they danced all night. They tell of walking home barefoot carrying their dancing slippers so as not to spoil the dainty shoes in the dust or mud of the unpaved streets. How good it felt too, to the feet tired from hours of dancing! There were many friends: the McKees, Dowsetts, Widemanns, McKibbens, Mists, Judge Hartwells, Atkinsons, Wilders, Judds, and Carters, to name a few, at whose homes the young von Holts and Mackintoshes had good times. Picnics and rides were always being planned. Marie recalls riding all the way to Waialua several times, stopping at Ewa for lunch, then at Leilehua at the Galbraiths' ranch for the night and on the next day.

One of Harry's memories was of his first bicycle, which, when he was learning to ride, caused a ludicrous accident. As he proceeded unsteadily along Judd St. he saw the old Chinese vegetable man jogging along with his two full baskets slung on a shoulder pole. Try as he would, he could not avoid hitting the poor man and knocked his baskets and vegetables in all directions. From then on whenever *Pake* saw Harry approaching, he would set his baskets down and hide behind the stone wall!

Grandpapa Brown died in 1886, so I only saw him once when I came to visit Marie while Bertha was in Australia, but I remember his kindly face and white beard very distinctly. Grandmama, or "Old Granny" as she was later called, was a beautiful woman, even when old, daintly dressed and always wearing a lace cap. My older children remember to this day the green glass jar of lemon drops which she kept by her side, and allowed the small visitors to sample. After her death in 1900, Little Mammy Mackintosh followed this custom.

Mrs. Mackintosh was always the greatest help to her husband in his parochial work, calling on and nursing the sick, helping out in any and all emergencies, generally known as a ministering angel and greatly beloved by the whole community. When she died in Dresden in 1904 a memorial service was held in St. Andrew's Cathedral which was crowded with young and old from all walks of life, all come to mourn the passing of their friend. The pew where she had always sat was banked with flowers and so many wished to express their love for her in tangible form that enough was given to build the beautiful tower of the Cathedral, while the family placed the pulpit to her memory and that of her father and mother.

After her mother's death Marie lived abroad for many years, returning to the islands in 1936, and has made her home here ever since, with her niece Alice Mackintosh. In

1938 she read the following paper at the annual meeting of the Daughters of Hawaii, which I include as being of interest:

"Many of you have read Isobel Strong Field's book called *This Life I Have Loved*. Well, if I wrote a book it would be called *This Life I Have Both Lived and Loved*, and these would be the extracts from it.

"In those days of yore when I was young, one would see Hawaiian men coming down Nuuanu Valley with large bunches of *Waiwai-iole* (mouse-foot) at Christmas time for our decorations. This was a mossy ferny plant very green and pretty, which is now quite rare. Then on looking up into the valleys one would see smoke rising from the woods, and we would know that charcoal was being made. This was brought to our doors for sale, in large *umekes*, for all our ironing was done with heavy irons with adjustable tops, or lids. These were filled with charcoal fanned to a flame until the charcoal was well lighted and the iron hot enough to use.

"Still another sight, which one never even sees in pictures now, was of men with long poles over their shoulders, carrying great bundles of grass, wound neatly round into shape about six feet high and four or five feet around. This was sold for our horses to eat, as there was no California hay in those days.

"Our fruit and vegetables were brought to the door by Chinamen who went jog-trot down the valley, calling in at all the neighbors to sell what they had grown themselves in the large gardens above us. Strawberries grew all the year round and were small but sweet. We were roused early in the morning by voices calling, 'Morning, Mama, you likee stlaw belly? Numba one stlaw belly, you come see.' Or one would call, 'Ducks, ducks, Mama likee ducks? Velly good ducks.' Guavas, too, were brought to the door for sale. No oranges were imported from California in those early days, but you may be surprised to hear that oranges grown in Kona, Hawaii, were exported to California! A few grown in

Waialua, Oahu, were often sold at the corner of Fort and Hotel streets, and there the good old Hawaiian custom of giving one *manuwahi* was the fashion, like the old English 'baker's dozen'. The Chinese brought guava jelly to the door for sale, so delicious and clear and rich in color that we thought there was none to beat it.

"Another sight to be seen was a Hawaiian carrying a single bamboo stick with rows of round tortoise shell combs stuck into niches. Those must have come from the South Seas, and how tidy they kept the children's hair when they went to school! Honey was brought to our doors by a very striking American man, of whom we were much afraid. His hair was long and he wore top boots and always carried a gun on his shoulder, and was followed by a pack of dogs. His was the only abode on the slopes of Punchbowl, just above the Queen's Hospital, and it was there that he kept his bees.

"One of the familiar sounds in the valley was the pounding of poi done by men sitting in the shade of the trees, with a large wooden trough, a calabash of water by their side, and a stone poi pounder. *Paiai* the hard stage of poi, was carried about and sold, carefully wrapped in *ti* leaves.

"There were only two carriages in Honolulu when I was very young, one belonging to the King, and one to Mr. Wood. The roads were very bad and rocky, and I well recall the bullock carts that drew rocks to mend them. I heard my first swear words from the bullock drivers, as they passed our home, 'Kahihuna,' on School St. near Queen Emma St. This was such a rough and muddy road!

"Saturday was a great day in the Honolulu of those days, as the natives came into town from over the pali and other parts of the island, wearing leis of maile, hala nuts, or kukuis, and all the women wearing *Pa-u's*, such a jolly colorful crowd. Some would be seen carrying awa roots, to make their favorite, but dangerous, drink, which tends to paralyse if taken too freely. On Saturday the Royal Hawaiian Band played in Queen Emma Square, which was a great place to meet all one's friends. The British Commissioner, Mr. Wodehouse, was always there, carrying his walking stick and greeting his many friends, and other notables were often to be met. 'The Dandy', a great character, with an eye-glass, a Stanley collar, white waist-coat, top hat, and very tight fitting trousers, was quite a sight. He often played the *Ukeke* as he strolled about between selections by the band.

"Wednesday was the 'Water Day' for our home Sunnyslope, when we could use the *auwai* exclusively. We first pumped the water into our tank, from where it was led into the kitchen and bath, and then we watered the garden. We had many wooden troughs which were stored in the carriage house, and on water days were hauled out and moved from spot to spot as the trees, shrubs and lawn needed it.

"And now as we are celebrating our dear Queen Emma's birthday, I must tell you of two very gracious acts of hers. My sister Bertha and I, with my brother Harry, were leaving for school in Portland, Oregon, in a sailing vessel, and the Queen invited the three of us to have tea with her in her home at the corner of Beretania and Nuuanu Sts. Before saying goodbye she wrote her name in our autograph albums, a page I treasure very highly.

"Another gracious act of hers was to invite the sister of the Bishop of Oregon (who was paying us a visit) to have tea with her at Waikiki. During the afternoon the Queen asked Miss Morris if she had ever tasted a fresh coconut. Miss Morris replied that she had never before even seen a coconut tree. Whereupon Queen Emma told one of her attendants to fetch down a good nut. The boy tied his feet together about a foot apart, to aid in climbing, climbed the tree, screwed off a nut and brought it to Miss Morris. She drank the milk and ate the meat, enjoying both very much. When she was returning to San Francisco, Queen Emma sent a parcel on board for her, and there was the very coconut she had seen picked, beautifully polished and made into a bowl."

CHAPTER VII

"Na Olelo o Ita me Hale"

IN 1881 Papa and Mama took the whole family to New Zealand for a year, where we stayed in Auckland for the schooling, but made many trips about the country. Mama was of course very happy to renew her memories of her girlhood in this lovely country, and to point out to her children the treasured spots where she and Uncle Frank had spent so many happy adventurous days. One of the especially memorable trips was to the hot spring country to see the famous Pink and Yellow Terraces. The water dripping down over wide ledges had left a most beautiful glaze on the rocks, in one place pink and in another yellow. Alas, these are no more visible, for a volcanic eruption destroyed both these terraces a few years after we had seen them.

Mama took us on a boat trip across one of the hot lakes, but Papa would not go, as he considered it very dangerous. Mama was always of an adventurous turn, and thought people who had things happen to them were foolish and did not take the proper precautions. On the other side of the hot lake the Maori boatman caught us a basket of fish in a clear little stream, then walking only a few feet, he cleaned them, put them into a basket with some new potatoes, and cooked them for us in a boiling spring. We children were much impressed, and thought both the fish and the potatoes the best we had ever tasted.

On our return from New Zealand in 1882 we found that there was an outbreak of the volcano at Kilauea, so my father decided to take us to see it. It took us four days to make the trip in the little steamer, as she stopped at all the way ports, but we finally got to Hilo, where we stayed with Dr. and Mrs. Kittredge while preparations were made for the long trip up the mountain, on horse back. We started off from Hilo at seven in the morning, and reached the Volcano House at six that evening, awfully stiff and weary after such a long ride over the *aa* roads. When we stopped at the half way house at Mountain View for lunch, we were much amused to see an old Hawaiian hurriedly catching a chicken, dispatching it, and popping it into the stew pot, but very tasty it proved to be.

The display at the rim of Kilauea was a grand one, as the lava was only seventy feet below the rim when we rode to the pit the next morning. The heat was so intense that we had to shield our faces with hats and coats in order to endure it. The lava, which was a deep fiery red, surged back and forth like ocean waves, first throwing up sprays of molten rock in the center of the pit, then at the sides of the cliffs, while the center would settle down and look almost smooth and closed over, as it cooled so quickly into black lava it seemed miraculous. After five or ten minutes the fire would burst out again throwing up molten lava near the cliffs and breaking into sheets of flame across the entire pit. Then the cakes of cooled lava would tilt themselves up like cakes of ice in a wide river and slide down into the fiery mass where all would be melted, and the pit in the wildest confusion. It is really too terrible and awesome to describe, and one feels face to face with the mysteries of creation.

Shortly after this the family went to Europe, where we remained for almost three years. During this time we visited Norway and met many of our uncles, aunts, and cousins, notably Professor Alexander Sieppel, of whom I have spoken elsewhere. We were in Berlin for a time, hearing lovely music and many operas, but most of our time was spent in Vienna, where the boys went to school, and I worked very hard with my music. The whole trip was a rich experience for us all, and meant much in our lives always.

On our return we spent some time in Honolulu, where we met for the first time many of our parent's old friends and their children. Dr. and Mrs. McGrew with Kate (Mrs. Charles B. Cooper) and Tarn (Tarn McGrew of Paris) welcomed us warmly, also the Frank Judds, Cookes, Carters, and others. One afternoon Mama and Papa took us to visit at "Sunnyslope" where we found the Rev. and Mrs. Mackintosh, Mr. and Mrs. Thomas Brown, and Marie von Holt. Bertha von Holt was then on a trip to Australia with Mrs. Pflueger, and Harry, who was working in W. G. Irwin and Co., was not at home. I remember liking them all so much, and feeling very complimented when Marie spoke of my silver grey dress. It really was awfully pretty and fitted me like the paper on the wall! Quite the latest thing! And I had only just begun to wear corsets, so felt very important and grown up! This was in July, and the following October or November Papa brought Maud and me up to town from Kauai. We were thrilled to be invited to Dr. and Mrs. McGrew's home, while Papa was to stay at the old Royal Hawaiian Hotel on Hotel and Richards Streets, where the Army and Navy Y.M.C.A. now stands. Great preparations went on to get us ready for our visits to the city, but finally we started off with Papa in our carriage and pair of horses, with two cowboys behind leading an extra pair. We took lunch along and ate it on the Lawai hills below the McBryde house, while the boys changed the horses. One boy then returned home with the tired horses, while we went on to Koloa, where we spent the night with Dr. and Mrs. Smith. Next day we drove the rest of the way to Lihue, calling on dear old Grandmother Rice, the Isenbergs, and Wilcox's, and having lunch with Mr. and Mrs. William H. Rice, the parents of Senator Charles Rice, and the rest of their big family. At five in the afternoon we were at the landing at Nawiliwili, where a crowd of people on horseback and in carriages were down to see the steamer off for Honolulu.

Papa got us in to one of the big whale boats, and though the surf was pretty high, we managed to get out to the steamer, and up the side of the bobbing vessel.

We girls were much intrigued to see a stout but fine looking Hawaiian woman come out in the next boat. She was a Chiefess of Lihue, and most stylishly dressed in a flowing black satin holoku and high black button boots. We were all agog to see how she would manage to get up the steep companion way to the deck. She solved that problem very neatly by absolutely refusing to budge from the boat at all! So the Captain finally had the sailors pull her up in the boat, and when at the deck level she was helped out with great ceremony. The jabbering and excitement, the auwe's, exclamations, shrieks of fear and of laughter, added to the general hubbub, but finally Her Highness was comfortably ensconced on the deck. When we went to our cabin later we saw her being regaled with fish and poi. It was rather a rough night, but we managed to sleep fairly well, until we were awakened about 1 A.M. with screams of "Someone over board," and the sudden stopping of the steamer. Out we rushed to the deck, to see a boat being lowered, and to discover it was our Chiefess who was overboard. She had become hot, and had gone to sit on the rail, and had toppled over in one of the sudden rolls of the tiny boat. Papa appeared, and we clung to him in apprehension of a tragedy. Would the lowered boat get to her in time? Would the engines in reverse perhaps hurt her in the turning of the screws? So many questions and fears, and all the Hawaiians on the deck in a great state of excitement. Suddenly across the pitchblack water came a faint "coo ee." We were all thrilled, and the Hawaiians exclaimed with delight "Pau ka pilikia kia! They will find her now!" And sure enough after some twenty or thirty minutes the boat pulled along side with Her Highness. She had had the presence of mind to take off her button boots, and her beautiful satin holoku, and had wrapped the boots inside the holoku, and was calmly swimming towards the boat. Never once had she felt dismayed nor thought she would not be picked up, and the sailors found her very cheerily swimming along in the middle of a rough channel, the wind blowing and the waves dashing over her. She was taken to a room by the Captain, and given some hot coffee, and we all went to bed again. The next morning the Chiefess was quite her usual self, all resplendent in her satin holoku and the high buttoned boots, which had been dried and restored to their pristine state.

We were so accustomed to the prowess of the Hawaiians in the water, and had heard so many tales of feats that I don't remember that we made anything of it, but later when we were on our travels we found that the story impressed people immensely. I remember another story of a man and his wife wrecked in their canoe between Diamond Head and Lanai. The woman swam the whole way back to Koko Head carrying her husband, who had been hurt, only to find on landing that he was dead. However she said she was thankful to have saved him from the sharks, and she had a bang up funeral with pomp and ceremony, and much loud wailing. A funeral to the Hawaiians to this day is on the order of a party, like the Irish wake.

We girls had a very jolly time with Dr. and Mrs. McGrew. Maud and Kate became great friends, and Mrs. McGrew helped us to shop, got a sewing woman and made us some new dresses, and even had me to one of her dinners. She put me next to Mr. W. G. Irwin, *aetat.* forty-five or so, which I thought very ancient. Mrs. McGrew told me to be nice to him, as he was a bachelor, and "a great catch." Of course after that I was completely tongue-tied!

One evening Papa took Maud and me to dinner at "Sunnyslope". I wore a light blue dress with little ruffles round the polonaise. My hair was then quite a Titian red, and curly, and I thought I looked rather nice! I shall never forget while sitting in the parlor talking to Grandmama Brown, (I could always get on beautifully with older people) dear "Little Mother" Mackintosh came up and said, "I want you to meet my little boy Harry," I looked up and up to

Harry Martens von Holt
1893

this tall six footer smiling down at me with big blue eyes and ravishing little sideburns. Something happened then and there to us both, for Maud complained I did nothing but rave over Harry von Holt the whole way back in the carriage, and long years afterwards Grandmama Brown told me that Harry came upstairs that evening and said to her, "If I ever marry, I am going to marry Ida Knudsen."

We were all happy and busy at home at Waiawa that year, Maud and the boys being tutored by a Mr. Marshall, a man of about thirty-eight who had been highly recommended to Papa on our way home through New York. He was not the first man Papa interviewed, that being a very good-looking young man by the name of Nash. Papa was very much impressed by Mr. Nash, and so were we girls. After he had left, Maud was eating some sweets, and Papa called her "my little Miss Nash-nash," the Norwegian words for sweet. Maud looked coyly at Papa, and said, "I'd rather be MRS. Nash-Nash." Papa looked very taken aback, said nothing, but we never heard anything more of the handsome Mr. Nash, and Papa engaged the awkward and ungainly Mr. Marshall, whom we youngsters all disliked. He was evidently clever in his teaching, however, for on our going to Boston in 1886 the boys entered their classes in Chauncy Hall School with no trouble. But what quiet fun we had out of school hours baiting the poor man! When he went riding with us we would tell him the most awful yarns, but we were too well brought up to be rude to him, and anyway we would not have dared to incur Papa's anger.

One of the thrills we had were the visits of the poor wee crazy Chinese woman who lived in Waimea Valley with some Hawaiians who were kind to her. She only spoke Chinese, and would suddenly appear, having walked all the five miles. She would catch hold of Mama's skirt, sink down to the ground, and wail and wail. Then she would jabber away in Chinese, and Mama would pat her head, we would bring mangoes, and she would wipe her eyes, smile, and be

Ida Elizabeth Knudsen
Bishop Museum Photo

comforted. Papa thought she felt our white faces seemed nearer of kin to her than the dark Hawaiians, and her loneliness and homesickness would come over her. It was said that when her husband or people returned to China, she had been left behind and so had gone crazy. She would go up on the Waimea cliffs back of the present Rectory, then the home of Governor Kanoa, and later his son Judge Kahu Kanoa, and scream and yell and gesticulate at her imaginary foes for an hour at a time. Mr. Marshall had seen her once, and one night Maud, who was a very good mimic, stationed herself in the dark near the door of the "Long House", as the guest cottage was called, about fifty feet from the main house. Mr. Marshall usually bade us goodnight about eight, and walked across the space which was lit by the lamps streaming through the door of the big house. Just as he was about to go up the low stairs of the cottage, Maud began to wail, and so good a rendition of the little Chinese woman's voice it was, that Mr. Marshall stopped one instant, then turned and fled back to Papa on the veranda. In fear and trembling he clung to Papa's arm, and would not go again to his room until Papa accompanied him, and got him safely in and the door locked. Papa assured him that she was harmless, and that he would see that she went away. We children were all perfectly delighted with the success of Maud's joke against the old tutor, but when she came out of her hiding place, we all felt she should own up, and we'd take our medicine if Papa was "hu hu." However, when Maud confessed, Papa just gave one amused look at her, and muttered "Jove, it was so like the old woman's voice you took me in absolutely, but," and here his voice grew stern, "I don't want any more of these pranks." We felt we were let off very easily, and next day Mama laughed about it with us, so we felt it was a huge success, and were terribly proud of Maud.

In the spring Mr. Marshall gave me a great shock. One evening I met him out by the water filter with a large glass of water in his long bony hand. He stopped me, and said,

"Miss Knudsen, would you do me the honor of becoming my wife?" With a horror-stricken gasp of "No" I fled. Maud and I often wondered what would have become of the glass of water if I had said yes!

There was much fun in our lives for Mama was fond of entertaining. Cousin Anton Faye and his wife lived near Kekaha mill. We saw a lot of them, also her brother Valdemar Borchgrevink who later was smitten by my charms, but I could not quite stand the thought of that name being mine all the rest of my life. "Knudsen" was difficult enough, and I had been called Cumsden and Nutzen and all sorts of other pronunciations. Mr. Brandt and Mr. Hofgaard were very good dancers, and with Anton and Hans Faye (my first cousins) kept a party going. Then we had Kate and Tarn McGrew to visit, and other young friends from town, as well as the McBrydes, Isenbergs, Rices, and other Kauai friends. It was always fun to go to Makaweli House where Grandmama Sinclair, tho then well over eighty, still took a great interest in the young folks. The Frank Damons and Henri McGrew came on a party up there, and we had a great time with charades and games. Of course we always went to Halemanu with our guests, and they loved the ride up the wonderful mountains, and how spell-bound they were by the boys' stories, such as Eric's ghost story of the time he was riding home quite late, and his horse suddenly stopped and snorted. Eric peered ahead into the darkness and saw a great white form standing in his path. Even as he watched, a long white arm swished up, first from one side and then from the other. The nervous tension became too great, and Eric yelled and spurred his horse forward . . . and a large white mule lumbered off the path!

This tale was followed by Augustus' story of 'The Smell of Dried Fish,' a fine ghost story with no explanation. Legend has it that an old Kalalau native used to come over to Waimea every so often to bring taro and dried fish to his daughter. On one such trip, which happened on the night of the full moon, he was set upon by thieves, and in the struggle the poor old man was killed. This took place near the Waimea Canyon rim at Puukapele. When the boys first heard this story they put no credence in the belief of the natives that the old man's ghost still waits at that place on full moon nights, but one evening when Eric was coming up from makai quite late, his skittish colt suddenly stopped, trembling and snorting, and refused to go on. Eric spurred the animal and it dashed across the dark swale, and coming up to the canyon rim at a good gallop, Eric saw the full moon rising over the edge of the mountains beyond. When he reached Halemanu and told his tale, he was laughed at, but a month later Augustus was riding home from a wild cattle hunt, with his dogs, and the same thing happened. The horse stopped and snorted, the dogs cringed and trembled with hackles raised. As he forced his horse across the same swale, Augustus smelled a strong smell of dried fish! and there, sure enough, was the full moon rising over the canyon rim.

Augustus also claimed to have seen a menehune on one of his camping out nights. He had been late hunting cattle, and built a fire to keep warm. As he sat eating chocolate and hard tack, he suddenly realized that across from him through the flames he could see a little figure, bushy haired and heavily bearded, and clad only in a malo, and about 18 inches high. When Augustus moved to try to see better, the little creature vanished, but he always believed he had really seen a menehune.

In 1886 when Harry, Marie, and Bertha von Holt came for a visit we had a most lively party up at Halemanu. The von Holts came over from the Valley House where they had been visiting the Spaldings. Rosie Makee (later Tenney) was there and was very fond of Harry, and began to call us "the Ka-nuisances" when they said they were going to Waiawa to pay us a visit! Harry was full of fun, as were Marie and Bertha, so we had a wonderful time. He had been taught by Queen Emma to dance the famous spear dance of Kamehameha I, and you children can all remember how splendidly your father did it. The foot action and the graceful rythm of arms and hands as he pantomimed the warding off of spears thrown at him by his warriors, was a marvelous sight. How I wish we could have had a movie taken of him dancing it as he did in the years gone by! Harry's fine baritone voice with Marie's accompaniment was also a pleasure. We all played and sang so much more than the present day young people. College songs, rounds, etc. were the rule after a picnic on the beach, or in the evenings. One of Harry's favorites was "Come into the garden, Maud" which he *said* he was singing to Maud, but he always *looked* at me! Another favorite was "Robin Hood," so we all organized a band of foresters. Harry was Robin Hood, Augustus Little John, and Eric Friar Tuck. They hunted and shot wild cattle, pigs, and goats, and had a most jolly time together. These nicknames stuck to them for years, Eric writing in the Kauai paper the "Garden Island," as late as 1930 under the nom de plume of Friar Tuck.

In the autumn of 1886 Mama and Papa took us all to Boston where the boys prepared for Harvard and M.I.T. Our life there was most delightful and of great value to us. We girls went to Miss Wesselhoeft's school on Marlborough St. Through Mr. and Mrs. James W. Austin who had lived many years in Honolulu, we got to know a number of delightful people. The Austin boys Herbert and Walter, (Herb and Wally) were awfully good to me and gave me lots of good times. I remember my first toboggan party which was great excitement and fun one cold winter evening. Then in the summers we rented the Admiral Harwood cottage, owned by his daughter. This was a charming place right on the water of Marion in Buzzard's Bay, with a private pier where we had two row boats and a small sail boat, called a cat boat, which Papa had built for the boys. They named her the "Ellida" after the boat in "Frithoff's Saga" in which the Viking sailed on so many adventures. This saga was one of Papa's favorites, and he was always quoting from it, in fact we had been practically brought up on Viking stories.

Miss Harwood would vacate her house by June 15th, and we would come down by train and fill the cottage. Five young people, from ten to seventeen, kept things lively, and we knew all the young folk around the little town. One day while I was digging around some plants in the garden I found a quaint old brooch which I carried to Mama. She immediately put on her hat and we walked over to see Miss Harwood. I shall never forget the look on her face when she saw the brooch. She took it in her two hands caressingly and said in a quiet low voice, "It has been lost for years. Oh thank you a thousand times, my dear, it means so much to me for my love gave it to me before he went to sea the last time. I never saw him again, for his ship was lost with all on board." She just stood there gazing at it while I pictured the whole tragic story. Then Mama and I slipped out, leaving her quite oblivious to our departure.

Mama organized Sunday evening "Sings," as we called them. Our room where the piano stood was quite large, with the stairs leading up to the second story. We had so many folk every Sunday that they sat all the way up the stairs as well as crowded into the room. I played a great deal as I was in splendid practice then, working sometimes six hours a day through the winter. We had Hymn books and all joined in singing for an hour at a time. Then Papa would bring in a crate of Delaware peaches which he always went up to the depot store to get every Saturday afternoon. Never again will peaches taste so delicious as those! We had bowls at intervals around the room to throw the pits into, and then one or two of us would pass bowls of water and old finger towels. Mama also always had lemonade and cookies, and a good time was had by all. When through the month of August our young clergyman, the Rev. Benjamin Brewster had the services, we always included him, as there was no evening service in those days. He thoroughly enjoyed the informality of it all, and added much as he had a splendid voice. All the girls were setting their caps for him, as he was goodlooking and only twenty-eight. He was of the original Brewster family of Mayflower fame, and was very clever and charming. However, though he used many persuasive arguments I could not forget my island boy, who kept sending me messages through Marie and Bertha, and birthday and Christmas cards. It seems funny now to think we never wrote to each other.

In the early summer of 1888 Mama decided to come back to see Grandmama Sinclair, and brought Maud and me with her. When we arrived at the Oakland mole there was Harry to meet us, much to our surprise. He had been offered a position through Mr. Henry Glade, so after resigning from W. G. Irwin and Co. in Honolulu he went to San Francisco, only to find that the position was not obtainable, the head of the concern saying Mr. Glade had misunderstood him. Poor Harry was awfully disgusted and mad, and almost returned to Honolulu with us. However he had an offer to go as freight clerk on the "City of Peking" to Japan and China, which gave him a good opportunity to see that part of the world. Before we left for Honolulu we had many lovely days together, one out at Golden Gate Park and walking on the sands at Seal Rock stands out in my memory!!

We became engaged that evening, and I sailed the next morning, and he to the Orient a few days later. We did not announce our engagement even to the family till we saw each other again in August when we returned to San Francisco on our way back to Boston, and happened to be there when Harry's ship came in from China.

We were not married until December 8, 1890, when Harry had a more secure position with the Oahu Railway & Land Co. The marriage took place in Boston, and we returned to live in the house on Judd St. which Papa had built for us for a wedding present, and which we called "Palikea" meaning "The White Stone," from the great rock in the back yard covered with white lichens. This was quite a famous spot, as it had been part of a heeiau in the olden days.

Here we lived many happy years, and here were born our five children, Mary Elizabeth on August 23, 1892, and named after her two great grandmothers who were both living:—Herman Valdemar on January 29, 1894, named for his two grandfathers:—Hilda Karen on January 21, 1897: —Ronald Kamehameha on August 11, 1898, called Kamehameha (the lone one), because he was the last child born under the Hawaiian flag:—and Katharine Anne on November 4, 1900.

In the early days of the Ranch Department of the Oahu Railway & Land Co., of which Harry was Superintendent, the outstanding need was for water for the stock, as the year before the ranches were taken over by the railway company a thousand head of cattle had died from want of water. Harry's first thought when out riding over the country was where to find water, and during the years 1890–91–92 much was done in the way of new troughs, getting water from the plantation flumes, and digging out wet places that showed any prospects of water. One of those places is on the old trail to Palehua, and had evidently been a place of which the Hawaiians had known, for its name is Kaloi (the taro patch), and even in dry weather water would be standing in the holes made by the cattle, as they tried to get a drop or two. An old Chinaman named Kin Lui, who had been a miner in California, was a splendid worker, and seemed to know just how to follow up any lead of water, and how to make a good tunnel. When water was finally led down the rocky hillside to the trough at Kaloi, Mr. William R. Castle, who was with Harry, rechristened the spring "Wai O Kakela," Kakela being Mr. Castle's Hawaiian name. But the old name still stuck to it, and as Kaloi it is known to this day.

One day as Kin Lui and his gang were digging there, and following the dribble of water, Harry noticed a green spot on the other side of the valley. Scrambling down through

Ida and Harry von Holt
with
Herman and Mary
1895
Bishop Museum Photo

the tall lantana, which was a veritable curse before the Board of Agriculture imported the lantana fly, he climbed up the other side of the steep valley and sat down under the shade of a projecting ledge to cool off. It was almost a cave, and can be seen plainly still. There while resting, and with his mind, as always, full of the subject of water, he suddenly saw a mud wasp, or mason bee, come in and add her little ball of mud to the house she was building on the roof of the cave. At once he thought, "Where that bee gets mud there must be water," so he watched carefully, and when she returned noticed that instead of coming from across the valley where the men were digging, she flew up and over the cave. In a few minutes he was trailing the bee, and soon found a muddy spot, where cattle had also made quite a boggy place by tramping about in search of a drink. Shouting to the men to come over with their picks and shovels, he soon got them busy clearing away lots of small stones and earth. Almost at once they could see that there were evidences of a paved well, and at about three feet down they came upon a huge flat rock, as large around as two men could span with their arms. Digging the rock loose and lifting it to one side, what was their astonishment to find a clear bubbling spring! Of course they were all delighted, and none more so than Harry.

On their return to the ranch house at Honouliuli that evening, it was soon spread around that "Hale" had found a new spring with much water. After supper, when he and Lui Warren, the foreman, were sitting on the lanai, two old Hawaiians who lived in the village and who were great friends of Harry's, came up, and after a friendly "E Hale, aloha no," they began at once to ask him about the spring, if he himself had found it, and whether he had ordered the stone removed. Harry at once sensed that something was wrong, so he asked "Pehea ka pilikia?," to which they answered, "Auwe! nui ka pilikia! You will die before the year is gone." Finally he got them to explain that the spring, called "Waihuna" (Hidden Spring) had been one of the

Harry Martens von Holt Family
Above: Herman, Mary, Harry, Hilda
Below: Katharine, Ida, Ronald
1901
Bishop Museum Photo

principal sources of water for all that country, which was quite heavily populated before the smallpox epidemic of 1840. In fact, there was a school for over forty children where the Stone Pen is now, below the forest planting. A powerful Kahuna living at the spring had hidden it before he died of the small pox, and had put a curse on the one who disturbed the stone, that he or she would surely die before a year was out. The two old Hawaiians were in such a state of fear that their beloved "Hale" would be "make," that Harry comforted them by asking if anything could be done to avert this evil curse. After a long confab they went home promising to do their best to help him.

Next day they came back, asking to have horses to go to Laie to see a woman there who was well versed in kahuna lore. So Harry gave them the horses, some money, and a bottle of okolehao, and off they started. Two weeks later they returned to report that the woman did not know how the curse could be broken, but that she had advised that they go to Molokai, where a very wise kahuna lived. So again Harry agreed they should go, paid their passages to Molokai, and supplied them with money and okolehao as before. In a month's time they were back at Honouliuli much elated, for they had found the kahuna in Molokai, and his "Unihi Pili," or familiar spirit, was stronger and more powerful than the "Unihi Pili" of the kahuna of the Hidden Spring and therefor could neutralize the curse. They told Harry that after a trance, in which the spirit of the kahuna on Molokai had been in communication with the departed spirits, he had declared the two old men could return to Honouliuli and tell their haole he would be safe, provided certain rites and ceremonies were carried out. First, preparations for a luau must be ordered, then Harry must go up to the valley behind the Hidden Spring, at the top of which the bird's nest ferns are so prolific now, and there he was to find a long tailed white rooster, a piece of awa root, and a black and yellow striped pig. "Well," said Harry, "I have seen white roosters up there, and I have no doubt that we can find some awa root, but I have never seen a black and yellow striped pig." However, he called out the cowboys and the pig dogs and off he went early the next morning to the designated valley. Soon they found the white rooster with the long tail, and some awa root, but no pig of any kind could they find, until late in the day, when the dogs gave tongue almost up at the head of the valley, and sure enough when every one arrived at the scene it was found they had cornered a black and yellow striped pig! So all was well, the luau was a great success, the departed spirits were properly propitiated, and the Hawaiians were happy to think they had been instrumental in saving their friend from death.

All this friendly interest, and partaking of their fears and superstitions, won for Harry the love and confidence of the natives, and he had consequently much help in finding the water which was so necessary to the work of the ranches, and for the starting of the forest planting all over the Waianae range, which Harry did for many years.

One episode in his hunt for water remains unexplained to this day. One day as he was riding alone on the lower slopes of the range, well below the spring Punahuna, his horse slid down a rocky bank, dislodging several large stones, and unearthing a trickle of water. Harry at once dismounted, dug around enough to see that it was a good flow, and marked the spot with a great pile of rocks, as well as taking careful bearings of the surrounding country. In a few days he found the time to return with Kin Lui and a few of his men, but though they all searched for hours, and Harry knew he was at the same place, no trace of the little spring was ever found, nor of the pile of rocks Harry had so carefully built. The only explanation he could think of was that this also was a sacred spring, and some of the Hawaiians when he had told of his find, had secretly gone there the next day and obliterated all signs. However, Harry had such success in general with the water that the Hawaiians regarded him as a water kahuna.

One of the greatest factors in our married life was the camp in the Waianae range, which began in 1896 when Harry was doing a great deal of work building the fence which now makes all of the tops of mountains a forest reserve. It was through his efforts that this reserve was established and experimental trees planted. Our children all remember "The Forestry" which Lui Warren called "Harry's monument." With memories of my happy days in the Kauai mountains at Halemano, I persuaded Harry to arrange for his family to also have a camp. He chose the flat land at Akupu, and we had several tents put up and spent a very happy six weeks there. Walter and May Frear were camping near by and May wrote many songs one of which "Pupu Kane Oi" she dedicated to Hilda. These were later published as the familiar song book "The Coco Palm."

Mary's first memory is of Akupu camp and of the seemingly great distance through tall dark koa trees to the Frear's camp. We all remember Mr. B. F. Dillingham, May's father, coming to stay with us, and his really talented snoring. While he was there a torrent of rain flooded the camp and we spent the rest of a wet night sitting on the kitchen table!

All water for Akupu was brought up from the Akupu Spring, which was carved out of the solid rock below the ridge, a distance of over a mile from camp. The little donkey "Mu" carried a large galvanized iron drum on each side of the pack saddle, and toiled up the steep grade twice every day.

In exploring the mountains we decided to move the camp to Pa Lehua because of the magnificent views, and the next year we built the present shack with the two big tents behind it. Few people realize what difficulties were surmounted in building Pa Lehua. Everything had to be carried by men on horseback or afoot from the edge of the cane fields at "29B." Imagine pieces of tin roofing, bundles of shakes, sections of the redwood tanks—coming up the narrow trail. I remember one windy day a piece of roofing was torn from the hands of the two men carrying it, and blown right over the ridge above Kaloi.

In those days we always rode from the ranch at Honouliuli as there were no carriage roads. Later on we drove to "29B" and took horses from there which saved us the long hot ride through the cane fields, but it still took us nearly all day, as we left Judd St. at 8:30 to catch the 9:15 train, got off at Honouliuli an hour later, walked ten minutes to the ranch house, and had early lunch there. Then on to the horses, and a two hour ride up into the hills, Harry always carrying the smallest child on a pillow fastened to a board he had ingeniously carved to fit over his pommel. Katharine remembers clearly leaning against her father's chest while he sang "In days of old when knights were bold." All of us remember singing "For bold Robin Hood and his foresters good" as we rode those beautiful trails. After getting to camp, beds had to be taken out and blankets from the camphor bags and all made ready in the two tents, with the lanai between.

One day at the end of our first six weeks we saw an old Hawaiian riding up to the gate. Harry called out to him in Hawaiian and he responded most affectionately, saying "Pehea ke keiki na kuahiwi?" (How are the children of the mountains?). Then he continued in Hawaiian "I will come and see you by and by, I want to go all around." Harry turned to me and told me the fine looking Hawaiian was Pekelo of Waialua, an old crony of his who had asked for a horse at the ranch to ride up and see the camp. After he had been gone about an hour Harry and I were sitting on the little platform in front of cabin when we saw him returning. When he got to the end of the platform he got down on his hands and knees and said, "E Hale, manao wao e Kahuna no oe." (O Harry, my thoughts are that you are truly a Kahuna.) Harry laughed his big jolly laugh and said, "Pele no paha" (Perhaps that is so). Then the old man crept up to Harry, totally disregarding me as well as Harry's remonstrances and taking Harry's hand, placed it

Twenty-nine B
On the Way to Pa Lehua

Pa Lehua, Waianae Mountains, Oahu

on his head, mumbling away in Hawaiian. Finally he sat back on his haunches, and told us that he had always had a suspicion that Harry had gifts of hidden power, and now he was convinced of it. Coming through the camp and examining the site of the house he had found a yellow lehua tree at the left north corner. All kahunas placed their mountain dwellings thus. Here was proof positive of all his surmisings. "Nonsense," Harry said, "I didn't even know there was a yellow lehua tree there." "Come and see," said the old man, so we got up and went around the corner of the house to look, and there it was with a bunch of yellow blossoms at the top! "Well," said old Pekelo, "It doesn't matter that YOU didn't know it. Many kahunas come back into different bodies and have the kahuna power without realizing it. Ever since you found the hidden spring at Kaloi, we have known that you had this power." It was characteristic of Harry's sympathetic nature and understanding soul that he never thought of laughing at the Hawaiian point of view. He loved the old folklore and ancient customs, appreciating all that was beautiful and spiritual and disregarding all that was not worthy.

After a good talk Pekelo had a big cup of coffee and condensed milk with hardtack, which all Hawaiians adore, and then departed, waving fondly to his "mountain children."

It is interesting to note in connection with this episode that the yellow lehua tree died after Harry's death.

Every summer we spent nearly two months at Pa Lehua. The children thrived on the camp food which they were never allowed at Palikea. Condensed milk, canned pineapple, Pa Lehua stew, cocoa, hardtack with butter and brown sugar were all great treats, as well as the many varieties of canned Australian jam. We always had two cows with their calves, the calves kept in a small pasture below the saddle house, where we also flew kites, and the cows coming up from the valley paddock twice daily to be milked by our faithful old Koegawa, Oda, or Kihara, who were our help and mainstay. The beloved nurse, Orai, guarded the babies. I remember the five children having their feet scrubbed in an old fashioned galvanized wash tub before going to bed.

There was little water, only that caught in the big tanks from the roof, and bathing was a luxury. We were allowed one bucket per bath—first soaped and scrubbed and then that icy water poured over us. No one believed a bath had really been taken unless piercing screams were heard from the little canvas bath tent, which was open to the sky. Once little Ronald left the horse trough faucet open all night, after watering the horses, and the tank was drained. We had to pack up and leave camp, so no one ever forgot again!

At night we went to bed by candlelight, and bed time stories were illustrated by shadow pictures on the tent walls. How good the red blankets felt in that cool night air, and how we loved the smell of camphor! We used bright figured calico sheets, which with the green or blue Japanese matting on the floor, and Japanese crepe "skirts" on the box bureaus—green with white storks and blue with white bamboo —made the tents seem gay. The main house had the dainty blue and white Japanese toweling at the windows and covering the shelves on the walls. The tables, built up there, had fringed burlap covers, which were replaced with delicate green ferns at meal times.

There were rustic benches made of lehua at all the views, where groups were always gathering for song and story. When looking at the lights of Honolulu at "the View" everyone was well wrapped in blankets as at that altitude of over two thousand feet it was often very cold. I remember once having the early morning temperature down to 46° and none of the children would get out of bed, until threatened with a cold wet wash rag.

When the children were still very small one of our favorite walks was up to Inspiration Point, and on to Elephant Rock, a noble formation shaped like an elephant's head with ear and eye sculptured by nature. Here many happy hours were spent with a queen in her howdah behind a mahout with his goad. Beyond Elephant Rock were some steps carved in a clayish soil where the smallest children played while the older ones were allowed to go over Gray Ridge. Little caves and houses were made in the clay, and here only were initials allowed. As Harry was nervous on foot on the cliffs he insisted on the children being tethered by bandanas tied through their overall straps until they became sure footed. No small child crossed Gray Ridge without this precaution. On these trails there were always little robbers attacking from behind every convenient clump of ferns, and many other imaginative games in the safe beautiful woods. There was an Indian encampment beyond Ferny Glen, where the bamboo forest is now, with tepees made of bagging and decorated with red paint. Mary was Nokomis, though she would have preferred to be Hiawatha —a role taken by Hermann—and Hilda was the beautiful Minnehaha. The greatest day was when George Carter allowed himself to be scalped, a huge success, as Hermann held aloft the toupee George always wore!

At Sunset View, nearer the camp, we often had hot supper, Pa Lehua stew and rice, and cocoa, carried up the trail by the faithful Kihara. The sunsets were usually spectacular and we made up stories about the beautiful cloud formations, and frequently saw Kauai, some ninety miles away across the channel. Harry used to sing "There's a heapa heapa trouble in de ol' man's mind, since Mary's gone wid de coon," and "Solomon Levi" in which we all joined. It was quite an adventure for the littlest ones stumbling down the trail to camp in the black dark. In recalling these experiences I am thrilled with the way history repeats itself with my little grandchildren following these traditions.

To help preserve the forests from the depredations of the many wild goats, hunting parties often used the camp. One of these included Mr. Harold Sewall, the American Minister to the Kingdom. He was impressed by the hunters' prowess on the cliffs, and tried to follow them. In spite of Harry's protestations, he climbed down the very precipitous face of the cliff near the great rock pile on the way to Green Peak, and when he came to return to where Harry was waiting for him, he found it was too steep and scary and he could not make it. After many tries, Harry called to him to go down into the small valley and take shelter for the night under the big trees and among the great rocks. He had his gun, his pipe and matches, so Harry left him. As it was growing dark by this time, Harry had to crawl over the ridges back to camp, as in those days there were no trails and one had to traverse the bare mountain.

On his arrival in camp to tell his tale, Old Kuhimana, the cowboy, was very makau (afraid) that the malihini would not be able to survive a cold night in the mountains, and finally persuaded Harry to allow him, with Arthur Mackintosh and George Potter who had just arrived, and were fresh, to go after Mr. Sewall, along the foothills. After many hours, they reached the place where they thought he must be, so they fired their guns, called and shouted, to no avail. They went on further, still calling and shooting off the guns. It was nearly impossible in the dark and foggy night to find the exact spot, and with no answer from the lost man, they were about to turn back when suddenly, far above them, came the sound of a shot. They climbed quickly up and found poor Mr. Sewall. He had used all his matches without being able to make a fire, so he was very cold and miserably wet. When he had first heard the rescue party, he had become so excited that he had jammed his gun, and in the darkness, had not been able to get it to work again until it was almost too late. He was very grateful to Kuhimana, Arthur and George, and made all the hunters vow eternal secrecy as to his foolishness. In a day or so I heard the story at a lunch at Helen Carter's, told by Mrs. Sewall, who thought it too good a tale to keep secret. From that time on that place has been called "Sewall's Leap."

Among these hunters were many beloved friends and relatives; Arthur Mackintosh, George Fuller, "Wish" Jordan, Al Castle, Hoby Walker, George Potter, and many others. We often had house parties with the young ladies awaiting the hunters' return, and great fun with songs, poetry and charades. The old guest book started in 1899 is a treasure of memories, and the new guest book, given to Pa Lehua by Hilda and Sherwood is well on its way as a record of many happy times.

As the family grew in mountain lore many picnics and rides were taken. New trails were built—"Over the Hills and Far Away," "Punahuna" to the tunnel, where one went in a long way with a candle, and where we all hunted for small kukui nuts; "Glen Ida" trail to Akupu, the "Golden Stairs" joining Glen Ida to the ridge trail, and the "Hog Back" trail where we went to watch the hunters, now Hermann and Ronald, Jack and Carter Galt, the Damons, and Pete Young among others.

Later on, the Schuyler Trail was built by old Peter, the black Portuguese from the Cape Verde Islands— a wonderful character who had been working on the trails and reservoirs since Harry's first days in the area. He was the one who made the famous remark to me, after a heavy rain, "You tell Hale that dam von Holt fool like Hell." I was puzzled until Harry explained that the new dam was named von Holt, and it *was* full! Peter also was the author of one of Harry's pet stories. On being told of the birth of the first baby, he said, "Good bleed, good bleed. Bool or heifer?".

The Schuyler Trail connected our mountains with Schofield, which was then called Leilehua Barracks, and was commanded by Colonel Schuyler, a dear friend. The children often stayed at Leilehua, having wonderful rides into the Kolekole Pass area, and loving the military life. In later years several young army officers used this trail to come for weekends at Pa Lehua, our girls riding out to meet them.

Our interest in nature was quickened by Montague Cooke's landshell hunts. He and Lila were among our frequent visitors, and Ronald went out hunting shells so often that he had a newly discovered type named for him. We found that each valley on the way to Green Peak had different colors and types of land shells, and land shell collecting enlivened our picnics and tramps.

When visitors were expected we always braided fern leis for the mantelpiece and door way, making the camp look very festive. Eloise and Ben Marx, Howard and Hessie Hitchcock with their family, David Anderson, George and Helen Carter with Bud, Phoebe and Robert, the Wilder children, Helen, Sam, Peggy and Alatau, Sue and Arthur Mackintosh with little Der, the Hedemans, the Castles, Alice and Teddy Cooke, Harriet Hatch, Beatrice Holdsworth were among the many friends often with us in this place of happy memories.

Another of the factors in our love of country was "Kikila," the beach property at Laie-maloo, so named because "Kikila" is the Hawaiian way of saying Cecil. This property came to Harry in 1917 from Uncle Cecil Brown, and in 1923 we made it into a place that has been a pleasure to us all, with room enough for all the children and grandchildren to stay and enjoy this beautiful windward climate. The swimming on both sides of "The Rock" is good, with surf and shallow water suitable for all ages, and the little ones can learn the art of body surfing in a safe place.

The first part came to Uncle Cecil about 1876, and was a small piece across the river from the present house. Uncle Cecil liked the peace and quiet of this then remote part of the island, and he was able to acquire several other pieces around the original holding. This land had been part of the Great Mahele, the granting of land to the Hawaiians as individuals, the deeds having to be signed by the King. Each Hawaiian according to his station in life received certain "kuleanas."

In Uncle Cecil's day there were many Hawaiians living on the place and all were good friends of their benefactor and companion "Kikila." The daughter of the original owner was his caretaker until her death, and I can still picture

Kikila, Laiemaloo, Oahu

her sitting at the top of the high steps to her cottage, smoking her pipe and surrounded by her children and grandchildren.

Some of the land was leased to Kahuku Plantation and there was cane all around the house, which consisted of an open lanai as a living room, with two bedrooms attached, a separate cottage with three bedrooms, and a cook house, all connected with a covered passage. The artesian well on the property was housed in a tiny building with a small swimming bath about eight by ten feet, and the water was always so cold that it required real courage to get into it.

With the cane cutting off the breeze, and with myriads of hungry mosquitoes, we found it an uncomfortable place to stay, though we did go over there once in a while. The first few trips we made we came by train to Kahuku, and then the rest of the way by the little plantation train, which dumped us, with all our boxes and bags, by the stone wall at the back of the property. After we got our automobile, about 1912, we came by road over the Pali, but the road around the island was in bad condition in those days, especially after rains, and the journey was long and tedious. At one place near Heeia it went down on to the beach, and could be negotiated only at low tide. Many a time we had to wait for the tide to go down in order to go on our way.

After Uncle Cecil's death it was decided to tear down the old houses, take out the cane from the beach side, and rebuild. When this was finally done in 1924, after a plan I had long wanted, the three houses were modeled after beautiful old Waiole Mission at Hanalei on Kauai, with the long sloping roof line simulating the Hawaiian roof of pili grass. The old bedroom cottage was taken to the back of the yard and remodeled into a guest cottage which we called "The Makule House." The artesian well was led to a new swimming pool where the clear limpid water is enjoyed by all. This water was always "free water," and the people who surround us used to use it, coming with their buckets on shoulder poles to carry it home.

In writing this story I have tried to put down the colorful and romantic history and background of our family, as my children and grandchildren have asked.

In conclusion I think it fitting to tell of a very vivid dream I had a few years ago, after the death of the little black Scottie Jock, the only dog I ever really liked. In this dream or vision I found myself riding up the trail to Palehua, and suddenly I heard Harry's lovely baritone voice singing his favorite song "Auhea," just around the bend of the trail. As I rode nearer the wee dog Jock came racing down the path, and I was just about to see my beloved Harry when, to my deep sorrow, I awoke. Some day I know it will be like that, and I won't wake up.

—I.E.v.H.

From the
HAWAIIAN CHURCH CHRONICLE
JULY, 1941

On June 20th. Ida Elizabeth Knudsen von Holt died at her home in Honolulu. In her death the Church in this diocese has lost a member who for deep interest and active service has seldom been equalled. Her many activities have left a deep imprint upon the development of Church and cultural life in Honolulu.

We are glad to reprint an editorial which appeared in the Star-Bulletin: "Few women in the community have had as varied, as wide, and as useful civic and cultural activities as Mrs. Ida von Holt, whose death a few days ago saddened her many friends.

"Church and other religious work: the Outdoor Circle, the former Footlights Club, the Community Theatre, the former League of Women Voters, the Morning Music Club, are subjects that suggest only a small part of the friendly and constructive work in which she was happily engaged. To her Honolulu owes a large part of its excellent standard of amatuer dramatics. Pa Hauoli, the little Theatre on Judd St. is only one expression of her sympathetic interest in music, the drama, public speaking. To this interest, Honolulu of the present owes a great deal, a debt of gratitude that will be shared by future generations."

Mrs. von Holt was also a charter member of the Y.W.C.A., and an active worker in that effective inter-racial organization in the islands. She was one of the first two women members of the St. Andrew's Parish Vestry. She was president for many years of the Guild and Auxiliary, and was Diocesan President of the Auxiliary for ten years, and her strong leadership was given to many other departments of Church life and activity.

A member of a distinguished island family, she was born at Waiawa, the family home at Kekaha, Kauai, the daughter of the late Valdemar Knudsen and Anne Sinclair Knudsen. As a girl, she was taken to Germany, where she studied music and art. Later she attended the Boston Conservatory of Music. On December 8, 1890, she was married to Harry Martens von Holt in Cambridge, Massachusetts. Her husband, also a member of a noted island family, died in 1927 while touring Europe. Surviving are five children, Mrs. Robert E. White of Honolulu, Mrs. Oliver B. Lyman of San Francisco, Mrs. Henry B. Caldwell of Lanai, Hermann V. von Holt of Honolulu, and Ronald K. von Holt of Kohala, Hawaii. There are also six grandchildren.

The quiet and impressive funeral service was conducted by the Rev. Canon William Ault, Mrs. von Holt's friend and pastor for thirty years. Never was the Cathedral more lovely in the variety and abundance and beauty of the flowers and leis which devoted friends from all walks of life sent as tributes of their affection and respect.

We can rejoice in the full and rich life of this faithful Churchwoman who more than rounded out the span of the traditional three score years and ten. We pray that she may be granted continual growth in love and service in the Heavenly Kingdom.

APPENDIX

All pioneer families disagree about the traditional tales inherited from the great grandparents about their former European homes. For those who love facts and are interested in the historical background, I recommend the local genealogical societies in Europe. They send you to parish registers, old army and navy records, etc., and tell you of the customs pertaining to your particular story that has been garbled or exaggerated over three or four generations.

My research into the Sinclair and Knudsen families, although incomplete, was interesting and rewarding. The two strangest stories are clearly explained and have become reasonable. The first is how Uncle Frank, our author's uncle, started the idea that he could turn down an earldom he was heir to. In "Armorial Families," by Fox-Davies, vol. 2, p. 1774, it states that the earldom of Caithness became extinct in 1889 with the death of a young unmarried earl. At that time a search was made for a near kinsman, and all the men of the Dunbeath branch of the Sinclairs were questioned about their position in the line of descent. The last two earls of Caithness had been from Dunbeath. No one was found and since then the head of the clan has been a baronet.

The wonderful story of the silver writing desk was explained to me by the Wellington Museum in London. Great men like Wellington were given enormous sums of money to spend at their discretion to commandeer any ship in the merchant service they needed for a special or secret mission. The navy records in London show no Francis or George Sinclair in their service. Since Francis was only 19 years old in 1815, he was probably with his father, George, of the port of Preston Pans, a registered "Master Mariner." That means he was a captain of one of the most seaworthy types of ships of Britain, since his run was from the port of Preston Pans near Edinburgh to London. His skill as a mariner must have been superb as that is a dreadful part of the North Sea. The historian in the museum told me that just such a ship and captain would be chosen by the Duke for a hurried journey from the continent if he wanted it kept secret. If he was particularly impressed with the captain, not only would he have paid the ship owner well, but also he would have given its captain just such an elegant gift in appreciation.

There is no tradition of Captain George Sinclair, our great great grandfather, having been knighted for this or any other deed.

      Ruth Knudsen Hanner
      1985

GENEALOGY OF
VON HOLT FAMILY

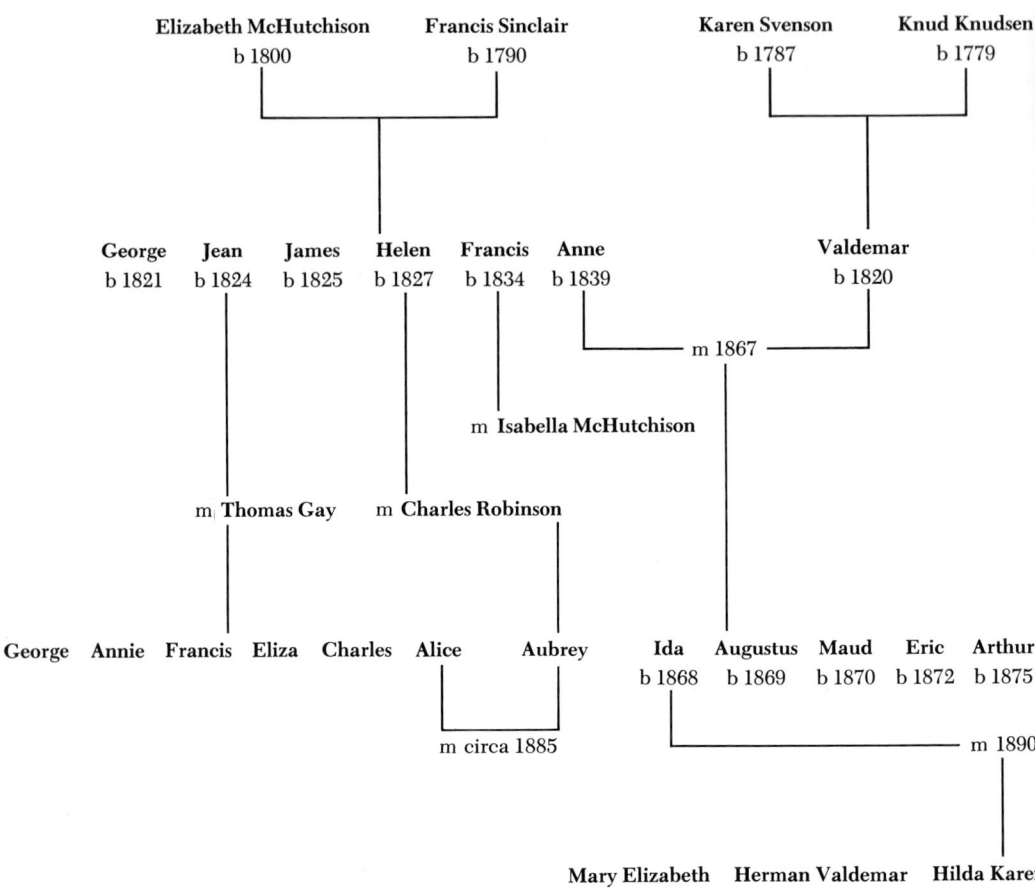

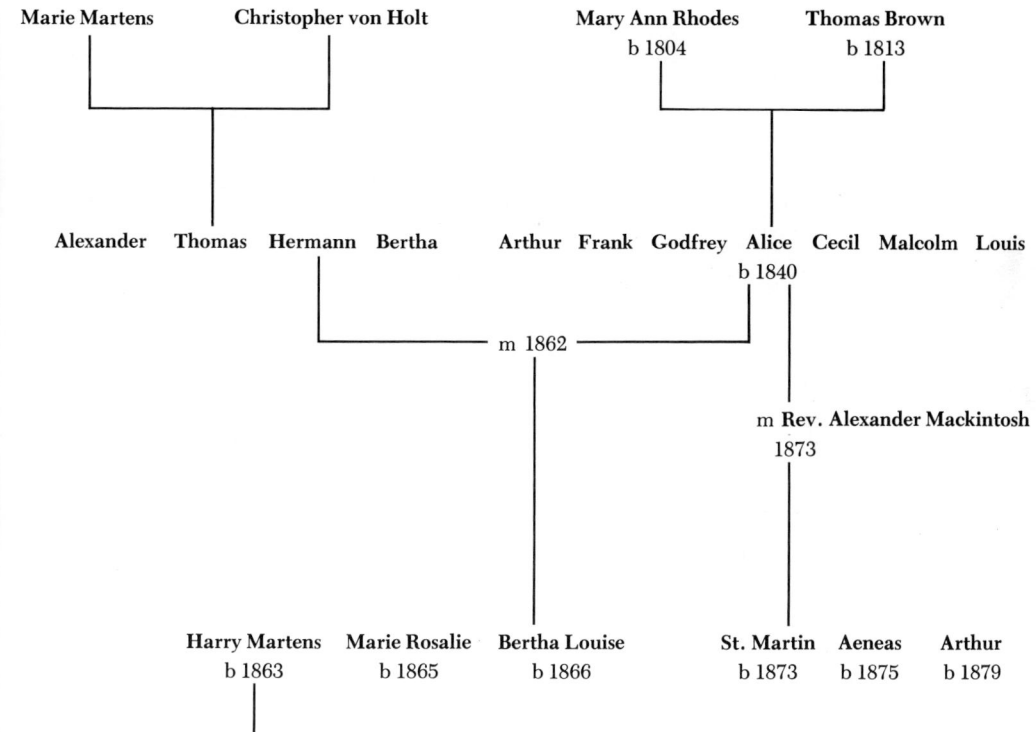